MW01708502

Sports Jokes & Trivia
with
Justplain Darren
and Friends

Sports Jokes & Trivia with Justplain Darren and Friends

ZEBRA

Published by Zebra Press
an imprint of Struik Publishers
(a division of New Holland Publishing (South Africa) (Pty) Ltd)
PO Box 1144, Cape Town, 8000
New Holland Publishing is a member of the Johnnic Publishing Group

First published 2002

1 3 5 7 9 10 8 6 4 2

Publishing manager: Marlene Fryer
Managing editor: Robert Plummer
Editor: Ronel Richter-Herbert
Cover and text designer: Natascha Adendorff

Reproduction by Hirt & Carter (Cape) (Pty) Ltd
Printed and bound by Creda Communications

ISBN 1 86872 663 0

www.zebrapress.co.za

This book is dedicated to the memory of Hansie Cronjé.
The mark of a true friend is someone who will stick with you through the good and bad times. I have no doubt Hansie would have done the same for me. Rest in peace, Spike.

Contents

Disclaimer

People will be stuck away in this book. Not least of all myself. As I am not taking legal action against anyone (despite not having vetted any of the submissions by the likes of Joel Stransky, Mike Haysman, Shaun Pollock and my fellow broadcasters (*sic*) on the Justplain show … and Walland) I expect the same courtesy in return.

This is a collection of stories, anecdotes, jokes, trivia and bits and pieces that have been sent to us over the past four years of the Justplain Show. It's a testament to the profile of the kind of listener that we have attracted. Most people think that only single-cell amoebas and plant life could listen to the drivel that comes out of the Justplain mouth, but, for some reason, we have an audience with an incredibly high intelligence index. In fact, most of my audience can do things that I have no clue about (e.g. surf the Internet, programme VCRs, speak proper English), and much of the material on the show is generated by the audience.

This book includes stories – both fictional and true – trivia and jokes that have been e-mailed to the show from you, the loyal fan. Maybe one of your e-mail submissions is even included somewhere in this collection. So, in many ways, this book is a tribute to you, the Justplain Loyal Listener.

It is also a small way of paying tribute to the sportsmen and women who make the sporting and entertainment aspect of the show so successful. Without the co-operation of icons – from Shaun Pollock to the late Hansie Cronjé, Bob Skinstad to Big Joe, Ernie Els to Lucas Radebe – and everyone who has given up a considerable amount of time to talk to us on our little radio show (sometimes about absolute crap!), we would have nowhere near the following that Nashua Sports Trax currently has! We can only say thanks, folks, for your contribution!

And thanks to our loyal sponsors such as Nashua, Samsung, Powerade, SAB, FNB and 365.com, Liberty, SA Rugby and SARFU, Standard Bank and the UCB, Ladbrokes, Michelin, Enforma, Wrigleys, Look & Listen and numerous others who have given up a lot of their cash to support the crazy stuff we do! Likewise our contributors: Ashraf Garda who makes sure that Baldrick sounds like he knows what he's talking about, Mike Haysman (the only Aussie we allow on the show!), Phil Liggett, Jake White, Joel Stransky, Ian MacIntosh, Nick Mallett, Neil Mallard and many many more. Many of these friends have given their personal input into this book as well … and probably stuck me away!

Not least of all, to my mates at 5fm, my home since 1996: the Boss Ant, the other boss Nick G (don't Grubb him up the wrong way – Baldrick's weak pun), John Langford and the marketing team, and my fellow DJs, especially F and Martinengo, whom I have been training as club DJs since 1997, and who are now bearing the fruits with much success! Thanks guys … You're my mates, and I will stand by you!

And last but not least, the team around me … Wazzup Ray, Leigh-Ann, Charl, Ed … oh yes, and Baldrick!

But most of all … this is for you, the loyal listener …

But whatever you do … don't forget the sunscreen.

JUSTPLAIN DARREN

Introduction

Why 'Justplain' Darren? It may not be the question I am asked most often, but it is asked quite frequently nevertheless! In this book I will reveal all! I will also answer the one question I am asked more than any other (from a radio point of view – so 'Where is Naas?' or 'What's on the other hand, Darren?' are two that I will ignore, as I have for the past five years).

That one question is: 'Is John Walland (Baldrick) really as dof as he sounds? And do you really hate him as much as it sounds like you do?' As well as answering that, I'll give a few insights into the other members of the Justplain team, as well as a few 'tit-bits' about Leigh-Ann Mol (née Van der Stadt).

Justplain

The show started as the Darren Scott Weekend Breakfast Show in 1986. This was after a three-month nightmare on the Coca-Cola Top 40 (nightmare for reasons that I cannot share for fear of dismissal). The boss decided to swap Ian F and myself around, and that's how I landed up having to wake up at 5.30–6.30 am every weekend to be on air from 7 to 10 am.

Normally I would wake up nearer to 6.30 am, and this was very often followed by another wake-up call from Steve Kirker (the DJ on air from 4 to 7 am) at around 6.55 am to find out where the hell I was. Ninety-nine percent of the time, the answer to this question should have been 'Still sleeping', but that just wouldn't do, and so began a litany of outrageous excuses as to why I was late for the show, which carry through to today (I still can't guarantee being on time at 3 pm). These include:

> 'The boom in our complex is jammed, I'm running late ...'
>
> 'My garage door is stuffed – I've called someone in, but ... I'm going to be late ...'

'I left home without my car keys and had to drive back to get them, so I'm going to be late ...'

'I've just landed in Jo'burg – my flight was delayed [at 7.00 in the morning on a Sunday??????]. So I'm running late ...'

'I've just run over my neighbour's dog ...'

A lot of 'clock malfunction' and 'car malfunction' stories were added to that. Ian F is actually compiling a list of excuses for my being late for the afternoon Justplain Show ... Perhaps the list is somewhere in this book as well?!!

Ironically, there was one legitimate excuse I couldn't use, because my previous efforts would have made it far too unbelievable and I would have been a laughing stock – but I actually had a legitimate reason why I was late one winter Sunday morning. I had actually got up on time, showered and dressed, and was in the car by 6.25 am – well ahead of schedule. That was until I came across an unfortunate water turtle stranded on its back in the middle of the road outside my complex. How it got there, I have no idea, but at 6.30 on a Sunday morning, there's no one else around to explain or assist, so I decided to come to the poor reptile's aid. It had obviously come from one of the streams or dams in my housing complex. I picked up the creature and, after it peed on me, put it on the back seat, drove to the dam and released it back into the wild! It scampered straight into the water without so much as an acknowledgement of thanks, and I never saw it again! By the time I was back on my way to the studio it was 6.45 ... and I was running late! No witnesses, no one to corroborate my story. I called in with the usual 'Hi, Steve, I'm on my way, running a bit late ... uh ... uh ... uh ... bloody garage door jammed again ... shit!!!! Play my first two songs and I'll be there by then ...!'

The sports guy on Saturday mornings was John Walland. He had been doing this gig since Moby Dick was a guppy, and that was the one drawback of getting off the chart show. (Actually the second – getting up that early on a weekend in winter is nothing to write home about!) Fortunately, Kevin Fine did sport on Sunday mornings, so I didn't have the overzealous, overbearing John twice every weekend.

Fine was fine … fairly competent, knew his sport and didn't run around the studio like Odie! He did have one irritating habit … leading every sports bulletin with tennis. He obviously has some type of leaning towards one of the world's, at times, most tedious sports. I kept asking him if it really mattered that some chick from the Ukraine with only one vowel in her name beat another alleged chick from Bulgaria with not a single vowel in her name. He felt it did …

Fine was also a little slow, as most Manchester United supporters are, and it took him three months to remember that we had added a couple of extra sports bulletins on Sunday mornings, and that he should actually be there for them.

Other than that, he was, and still is, OK …

But Walland … let the truth be told.

John Walland

To answer the popular question: no, he's not dof, but god, he could've fooled millions!!!!

The banter started on Saturday mornings. At first I would sit in stunned silence at some of his pronunciations. Then I realised that, half the time, he had no idea who he was talking about, and so I began to speak up. The more you challenge John about some or other sporting issue or point of reference, the more he will try to argue that he knows what he's talking about, and the bigger hole he will dig for himself. By now that hole is so big, he could come crashing through the field surface at any time during the next Aussie Tri-Nations game or cricket Test at the MCG!

I'll give him one thing … he certainly can harass any sports person into giving us an interview. I'll grant him that. You see, he has this book. I call it ‘the book of harassment’. In it is every sportsman and woman’s phone number from the beginning of time! He takes it everywhere – toilet, bed, Teazers, you name the place, that book never leaves his sight. The new game between Ed (the engineer) and myself is to try to steal the book and hide it. For entertainment value alone, this is a great game. Baldrick literally goes into a state of panic. He sulks, whines, notifies the entire SABC management no matter what time of day or night … If he could, I am sure he would declare a national state of emergency … It’s hilarious!

When the boss put in the transfer request moving me from weekend breakfast to afternoon drive, Walland had become something of an institution on the breakfast show. Joining up with Glenn Hicks for the first couple of months of sports hour (Nashua Sportstrax) was great from a credibility point of view, but I felt that the show needed the Saturday morning vibe that came from the jibing, fun-poking and bickering that Walland provided. The boss agreed, and John moved to the afternoon to take up his residency as the show’s village idiot.

One question I am often asked is how John got the nickname Baldrick. This nickname hit me like a ton of bricks one weekend when I purchased the entire *Blackadder* TV series on DVD. I had my own private ‘*Blackadder* festival’ at home, and within three minutes of watching one of the first episodes, it struck me: watching Blackadder and his trusty but browbeaten sidekick Baldrick was like watching 3–7 pm in the 5fm studio! Baldrick was Walland, and Walland was Baldrick! I decided there and then to test it on the show the following Monday: ‘And now with the sports heads, what you got Baldrick …?’ Ray White, Ed and the producer of the day all fell about in fits. Only Baldrick himself didn’t know what the hell I was going on about. He hadn’t watched *Blackadder* or didn’t even know who or what it was … It could’ve been the Bok tight five for all he knew … But the rest had, and it stuck from that day onwards.

He still maintains that he knows nothing about Blackadder or Baldrick, but the rest of us know that he probably rented one or two videos of the series within a day or two of adopting his new name, and knows exactly what we're talking about!

Having said that, Baldrick has endured much over the four years of Justplain Shows so far. And maybe it's time the truth be revealed about some of the challenges we have put up that poor old John continually loses.

For one, the constant argument about the Comrades – that he has only successfully completed nine, and cheated in his tenth by climbing onto the back of a Coke truck (which, in a set-up, was falsely corroborated by many a Comrades legend) – is actually a lie. He did get his green number and did run ten, but the joke gave us many a week of pleasure. It caused Baldrick so much anxiety that he went and ordered an entire wardrobe of Comrades' attire and badges to prove his innocence. He was a bit distraught when he arrived at an outside broadcast one day in his green number shirt (given only to runners who have run ten Comrades) to find yours truly sitting at the desk wearing exactly the same shirt! I knew one of the organisers, who was willing to play along!

The infamous weight-loss challenge – which resulted in Baldrick having to stand on a street corner in Cape Town with a sign stating 'I'm John, I'm fat, please help!' – was also a con! With help from Ed and a few weights and adjusted numbers here and there, we managed to convince Baldrick that while I had lost 17 kgs (I had actually only lost about 7) he had in fact put on 2 or 3 kgs (he had actually lost about 10), and thereby lost the challenge!

Then there was the time Ray and I had a squash challenge before a Newscafe roadshow, where the loser of the game would have to sit through the entire show wearing women's clothing. Well, that was also a bit of a double whammy on Balders! You see, John felt safe with this bet … he wasn't even involved. It was a straight fight between Ray and me. Whichever of us lost the squash challenge would have to dress up in drag for the show at the Newscafe. Ray hammered me in straight games. On the way to the show, I had to come up with a cunning plan to avoid wearing the dress … but Ray wasn't going to let me off this one for anything! But then I told him what the cunning plan was: we would say that the match was a tie, and according to the show's (non-existent) rules, in the case of a tie, Baldrick would have to wear the women's clothes. Ray loved the idea, and Baldrick spent the entire show at a packed Newscafe (in Bloem, remember) with a size 32 dress on his size 46 body!

But it's not all my doing all the time. Very often my phone rings with a sports person or other celebrity giving advice on how to scam Baldrick with some or other scenario. The best one of all was when John went on our Supersaturday TV show and predicted an England win over South Africa in a One-Day International cricket match. On the Monday after, Shaun Pollock phoned me in the morning suggesting that we phone-scam John ... I would record Shaun (who was lined up for an interview that evening) phoning John and crapping all over him about how disloyal he was to South African cricket and saying that, as a result, he never wanted to be interviewed by him again! The call was a pearler, and John was totally distraught until he found out it was only a scam!

But to answer the much asked question: no, he's not as dof as he comes across; yes, he can be gullible; no, he isn't the world's greatest encyclopaedia on sport; yes, he does have the sympathy vote on the show that makes anyone who hasn't pulled the wings off a fly before want to hug him and spit at me; no, I don't hate him, despite the fact that I want to throw that bloody copper ashtray at him sometimes and probably still will ... and, yes, he definitely is Baldrick! Part and parcel of the Justplain Show!

Ray White

The Benoni breker considers the Justplain Show to be his second favourite programme on 5fm! He has a very close (and suspicious) relationship with Mark Pilgrim on a Saturday and Sunday morning, and we on the Justplain Show don't particularly want to mess with budding romances. This almost went sour when André the Hilarious Hypnotist put Ray under on one particular show, and Ray started spading Baldrick! Fortunately, we got him out of it before he could rip a traumatised Walland's clothes off, but not before Ray came out with his love for the Backstreet Boys, and the revelation that he was actually Britney Spears!

Ray's been doing news on the show since we started, alternating with Leigh-Ann van der Stadt/Mol. He loves the Weekend Blastoff, so it was fitting that just recently Ray put the challenge to us that if Elvis Presley got to No. 1 on the Hi 5 (with the song 'A Little Less Conversation' – Ray's favourite for 2002) he would dress up in his Elvis outfit which he's been storing in his closet since 1977 when Elvis died (the fat Elvis suit, that is – wig and all!). Elvis did in fact make it to No. 1 the following Friday, which meant that Ray would get into his Elvis drag the next Friday for the Weekend Blastoff. What Ray didn't realise was that that particular Friday was a Weekend Blastoff roadshow at Newscafe, Menlyn in Pretoria! Our Ray White is now an official and public Elvis impersonator!

A fact you didn't know: he has a batman tattoo on his upper arm and will remain on the show until his daughter Chloe is old enough to date me …

Leigh-Ann Mol

Leigh-Ann has grown up nicely – veeeeerrrrryyy nicely – since the Justplain Show started! Because she is the only girl amongst all the guys, we go out of our way not to be chauvinistic, sexist or make rude comments or remarks about things like her breasts, and give her the leeway at all times to give her point of view on the show.

But one personal observation: she is dyslexic!

Dyslexic in a sweet way, because, despite her average 3,6 mispronunciations per news bulletin, no one to this day has phoned or e-mailed to complain. I am convinced that her name is actually 'Anelle Lom' and her maiden name was actually 'Daestervan' (Dutch). She has had a few crackers, but none better than the rugby player Steyn Swart who 'allegedly faked his own appearance' – as opposed to disappearance!!!

Leigh-Ann is a mine of information, and although she loses most, if not all, arguments on the show, she is always there when you want to remember a particular commercial jingle or even a song. Don't ask her to identify artists or bands, though ... One particular incident that comes to mind is when she introduced the Red Hot Chili Peppers as Frank Sinatra! Actually, she said 'Srank Finatra', but you know what I mean ...

At this point we must take issue with the tone-deaf Ed Jordan, who failed our own Leigh-Ann after we had trained her and entered her in the Coca-Cola Popstars contest! How Jordan could fail her just because she did a Barry White version of Atomic Kitten's 'Whole Again', I will never understand. And she wore her nurse's outfit at the audition as well (another one of those things you find in newsreaders' closets.)

Check out the newsroom's submission of other dyslexic crackers that have made it onto the show, many of which can be attributed to our favourite female presence on the show – with apologies to Baldrick.

The producers

Now and again, you may have heard the odd strange name pop up as part of the team. There was Rui, Sonny, then Perky, then Graham, and now Charl. These are the people that are affectionately known on the show as the 'soon-to-be-fired producers'. As Paul Hardcastle would have written: the average stay of a producer on the Justplain Show ... is 19 days! Current producer Charl Erasmus is about to better that average ... good luck Charl!

Ed!

Another favourite question ... Who the hell is Ed!!!??? Ed is our engineer. The engineer is the guy who sits in the canteen at the SABC for four to six hours a day, drinking coffee, chatting to SABC TV presenters and other engineers, and who is kitted out with the latest Leatherman. When something breaks in the studio, the engineer's duty is to acknowledge that something is broken and order another cup of coffee. Now and again the Leatherman will make its way into the studio, accompanied by the engineer. This normally occurs only when a swimwear model happens to be in the studio at the time. Then the engineer will not only fix the problem, but everything else in the studio that isn't broken yet. The best way to get Ed into the studio when something is broken is not to phone Ed, but to phone Megan McKenzie and invite her to the studio.

Ed's name is actually $&*!@^&% [censored by Ed]. He is sometimes called DJ Ed, because he anoraks Sasha Martinengo and Mark Gillman when they go out to do club gigs. People at clubs actually think Ed is a DJ. Ed actually gets his name from the *Lion King* movie. You will remember that Ed was the hyena who got into a scrap and ate his own leg – the dof one. Well, our Ed isn't dof … he was actually named after a hyena because whenever we have even the hint of a good-looking woman near the ground-floor studio, Ed, who might be on the eighth floor at the time, will arrive at the studio within minutes, without being called or told. Much like a hyena in the Serengeti who can sniff prey from kilometres away. Hence the tag of Ed!

Of course, when that girl happens to be Megan McKenzie, then Ed will chew off his own leg!

So … Justplain?????

The name actually evolved after a couple of months on the drive show. I always tell folks that I call myself this so that no one expects too much … After all, how much can you expect from someone who is 'Justplain'?

But that's not the full story …

I've actually had the tag up my sleeve since 1992, but the afternoon show was the first ideal opportunity to unleash it! And where did it come from?

If I told you … I'd have to kill you …

Justplain Darren & Friends Profile
Darren Scott

Favourite personal sporting memory?	Smashing Rod McCurdy all over Newlands in front of 30 000 people in between a Standard Bank semi-final match. Included in that 22-run over was a reverse-sweep four off a bouncer, three cover-drive fours, and one charge, as arranged over a bottle of port beforehand!!
What's your idea of a perfect weekend?	Some time at my home in the bush; a few hours at Rhapsody; a minimum of 20 suitcases; a few Jacks; a Springbok victory; any Aussie loss; and Baldrick away on leave
What would be the best way for a fan to approach you in a bar?	Any line that doesn't have the name 'Naas' in it!
What do you refuse to pay for?	Sex, or my bill at Rhapsody
Tell us a secret of your trade?	If you want something done properly, kill Baldrick before you get started …
Have you ever been arrested? And for what?	Yes … for impersonating a club DJ. I'm on a suspended sentence …
What's been the lowest task/job you've ever had to perform?	Travelling to Malaysia and then Zanzibar for the Nashua *SA Sports Illustrated* swimwear edition photo shoots … Hanging around these places for a week at a time, with bikini-clad swimwear models running around, is just not on …
What will always be in your fridge?	Passion fruit … you never know when an emergency suitcase might be needed. Also, that 1 X head of lettuce that I keep throwing away … it keeps coming back!
Favourite 'junk food' meal?	McDonalds Quarter Pounder Deluxe, large fries, SUPER-SIZE!!!!

What's the last drink you have before going to bed at night?	The last drink (Jack) normally means I DON'T get to bed at night!
What's your biggest indulgence?	My new home in the bush!!! Magaliesberg mountains on one side, Hartebeespoort Dam on the other, and bush and wildlife all around ... eat your heart out, Cape Town!
Best advice given to you by your mother?	Are you sure about getting married ...?
What would your profession be if you were not a professional radio DJ?	Ripping off the decks on the one-one-two's playing uplifting home as a cutting-edge club DJ! (If my parole officer is reading this ... only joking!)
There are Seven Wonders of the World, what's your eighth?	Leigh-Ann Mol (actually ... that's eight and nine!)
Your Top 5 list of music?	Robbie Williams Robbie Williams Robbie Williams Robbie Williams Robbie Williams
Best 'chirp' you have heard during a sports event?	Terry Venables during the World Cup after Brazil slotted a free kick against China: 'You'd have thought that at least the Chinese could build a better wall!'
Who is your mentor/hero?	Ayrton Senna, David Letterman, Robbie Williams, BIG JOE!!!!
If you could swap places with anyone for a day who would it be, and why?	Sasha Martinengo ... Paula is such a babe. Otherwise ... Ray White ... Chloe is such a babe!
A quote or phrase that has had an impact on your life or best describes you?	'For God's sake, Darren, we don't have a job for you, now f**k off!' – Stuart Lee 604 – 1984
A one-liner that best describes your radio show?	'Sorry Ian, I'm running a bit late ... won't you start my first few songs ...?'

Read the following six statements and the amazing conclusion they lead to:

1. The sport of choice for the urban poor is BASKETBALL.
2. The sport of choice for maintenance-level employees is BOWLING.
3. The sport of choice for front-line workers is FOOTBALL.
4. The sport of choice for supervisors is CRICKET.
5. The sport of choice for middle management is TENNIS.
6. The sport of choice for corporate officers is GOLF.

The amazing conclusion: The higher up you are in the corporate structure, the smaller your balls become. This may explain why women are taking over the corporate world.

Great Sporting Quotes

'This is a really lovely horse. I once rode her mother.'
– Ted Walsh – horse-racing commentator

'Moses Kiptanui – the 19-year-old Kenyan who turned 20 a few weeks ago.'
– David Coleman

'I've never had major knee surgery on any other part of my body.'
– Winston Bennett

'Sure there have been injuries and deaths in boxing – but none of them serious.'
– Alan Minter

'The racecourse is as level as a billiard ball.'
– John Francombe

'Ah, isn't that nice, the wife of the Cambridge president is kissing the cox of the Oxford crew.'
– Harry Carpenter – BBC TV – Boat race 1977

'... and later we will have action from the men's coxless pairs.'
– Sue Barker

'Here we are in the Holy Land of Israel – a Mecca for tourists.'
– David Vine

'Morcelli has four fastest 1 500-metres times ever, and all those times are at 1 500 metres.'
– David Coleman

'Her time is 4:33, which she's capable of.'
– David Coleman

Dennis Pennis 'Have you ever thought of writing your autobiography?'
Chris Eubank 'On what?'

'There goes Juantorena down the back straight, opening his legs and showing his class.'
– David Coleman at the Montreal Olympics

'And for those of you who watched the last programme (Fanny and Johnny Cradock), I hope your doughnuts turn out like Fanny's.'
– David Coleman at the start of Match of the Day

‘Once Tony Daley opens his legs you’ve got a problem.’
– Howard Wilkinson

‘It’s a great advantage to be able to hurdle with both legs.’
– David Coleman

‘And with an alphabetical irony, Nigeria follows New Zealand.’
– David Coleman

‘Fred Davis, the doyen of snooker, now 67 years of age and too old to get his leg over, prefers to use his left hand.’
– Ted Lowe

‘I was in a no-win situation, so I’m glad that I won rather than lost.’
– Frank Bruno

‘Henry Horton’s got a funny stance. It looks as if he’s shitting on a shooting stick.’
– Brian Johnson

‘There’s going to be a real ding-dong when the bell goes.’
– David Coleman

‘There is Brendan Foster, by himself, with 20 000 people.’
– David Coleman

‘She’s not Ben Johnson – but then who is?’
– David Coleman

‘Watch the time – it gives you an indication of how fast they are running.’
– Ron Pickering

‘The French are not normally a Nordic skiing nation.’
– Ron Pickering

‘That’s inches away from being millimeter perfect.’
– Ted Lowe

‘Bobby Gould thinks I am trying to stab him in the back. In fact, I’m right behind him.’
– Stuart Pearson

‘I’ll fight Lloyd Honeyghan for nothing if the price is right.’
– Marlon Starling

‘I can’t tell who is leading – it’s either Oxford or Cambridge.’
– John Snagge, referring to the Boat Race

‘Sex is an anti-climax after that!’

– Grand National-winning jockey Mark Fitzgerald

‘Well, you gave your horse a wonderful ride, everybody saw that.’

– Desmond Lynam

‘Ardiles strokes the ball like it is part of his own anatomy.’

– Jimmy Magee, RTE

‘What do you have when you’ve got an agent buried up to his neck in sand? Not enough sand.’

– Pat Williams, US basketball player

‘Hair like badly turned broccoli.’

– Clive James, Australian broadcaster, referring to John McEnroe

‘Muhammad Ali isn’t a puncher. He just hit me so many times I didn’t know where I was.’

– Brian London, British heavyweight boxer

‘The man who will whip me will be fast, strong and hasn’t been born yet.’

– Muhammad Ali

‘When you are as great as I am, it’s hard to be humble.’

– Muhammad Ali

‘Putting a fighter in the business world is like putting silk stockings on a pig.’

– Jack Hurley, US boxing promoter

‘I’ve got ten pairs of training shoes. One for every day of the week.’

– Samantha Fox, British model and pop singer

‘I leapt at the tape like a man taking his last spring to save himself from the chasm that threatens to engulf him … I felt like an exploded light bulb with no will to live.’

– Sir Roger Bannister referring to the moment he broke the four-minute mile in 1954

‘There’s no skill involved. Just go up there and swing at the ball.’

– Joe DiMaggio referring to baseball

Justplain Darren & Friends Profile
John Walland

Favourite personal sporting memory?	Kneecapping a caddy the very first time I let loose with a driver at golf. Otherwise, the time I actually got through an entire sports bulletin without cocking up once (i.e. Darren didn't crap on me once for anything!)
What's your idea of a perfect weekend?	Getting locked in a changeroom with the Springbok rugby team. (Also qualifies as the Springboks' biggest nightmare weekend)
What would be the best way for a fan to approach you in a bar?	Well, I normally only go to gay bars, so a simple 'helloo big boy' would be enough …
What do you refuse to pay for?	Anything!
Tell us a secret of your trade?	The less you know about sport, the longer you stay in the job!
Have you ever been arrested? And for what?	Yes … Once for trying to break into the Big Brother house, and the other time for impersonating a human being
What's been the lowest task/job you've ever had to perform?	Sport on the Gillman Show
What will always be in your fridge?	Toilet paper, and Cokes stolen from the 5fm fridge
Favourite 'junk food' meal?	Anything with a greasy sausage in it
What's the last drink you have before going to bed at night?	My sex life is personal!!

What's your biggest indulgence?	Harassing people for free stuff
Best advice given to you by your mother?	Wash your hair every day or you'll go bald
What would your profession be if you were not a professional radio presenter?	I'm not a professional radio presenter anyway, so that's what I'd like to be
There are Seven Wonders of the World, what's your eighth?	The Springbok tight five, the Protea opening batsmen … and my eighth would be Okkert Brits
Your Top 5 list of music?	Showaddywaddy Smokie The Bay City Rollers The Sweet Lulu
Best 'chirp' you have heard during a sports event?	'95 World Cup … 'Oh for f***ks sake Stransky, pass the bloody ball … Hennie's ope …'
Who is your mentor/hero?	Justplain
If you could swap places with anyone for a day who would it be, and why?	The Construction worker from the Village People … great outfit!
A quote or phrase that has had an impact on your life or best describes you?	Shut up Baldrick!
A one-liner that best describes Darren and his radio show?	Shut up Baldrick!

General Sports Trivia

1. In which city is the largest sports stadium?
2. Which single race is the richest in the world?
3. Who was the first athlete to run a sub-four-minute mile?
4. In how many fights did Muhammad Ali box as Cassius Clay?
5. Who was the youngest person to have won a Wimbledon singles title?
6. Badminton is usually played to 15 points. When is it played to 11 points?
7. Which Open could Ivan Lendl never win?
8. What career did Sebastian Coe pursue after his retirement from athletics?
9. Who has won nine successive New York marathons?
10. In which sport do the players wear their numbers on their heads?
11. What is the only sport played with mixed teams, with four men and four women?
12. Who won the first world heavyweight title fight scheduled for 12 rounds?
13. How old are the trotters that run in the Hambletonian Classic?
14. Where is the White Sox baseball team's home ground?
15. How many goals did Wayne Gretzky score in the 1981–1982 hockey season?

Answers to GENERAL SPORTS TRIVIA on page 31

Fast Sporting Facts

Sports command the biggest television audiences, led by the Summer Olympics, World Cup soccer and Formula One racing.

Soccer is the most attended or watched sport in the world.

Fishing is the biggest participant sport in the world.

More than 100 million people hold hunting licences.

Boxing became a legal sport in 1901.

Jean Genevieve Garnerin was the first female parachutist, jumping from a hot-air balloon in 1799.

In 1975 Junko Tabei from Japan became the first woman to reach the top of Everest.

The first instance of global electronic communications took place in 1871 when news of the Derby winner was telegraphed from London to Calcutta in under five minutes.

In 1898, one of the first programmes to be broadcasted on radio was a yacht race that took place in British waters.

Gymnasiums were introduced in 900 BC and Greek athletes practised in the nude to the accompaniment of music. They also performed naked at the Olympic Games.

Michael Schumacher is the highest paid sportsman, ahead of Tiger Woods and Arnold Palmer. (Not including sponsorship endorsements.)

Martina Hingis is the highest paid sportswoman.

The high jump method of jumping head first and landing on the back is called the Fosbury Flop.

About 42 000 tennis balls are used in the plus-minus 650 matches in the Wimbledon Championship.

The Major League Baseball teams use about 850 000 balls per season.

A baseball ball has exactly 108 stitches, a cricket ball has between 65 and 70 stitches.

A soccer ball is made up of 32 leather panels, held together by 642 stitches.

Basketball and rugby balls are made from synthetic material. Earlier, pigs' bladders were used as rugby balls.

The shuttlecock is one of the fastest objects in sport. It travels at an average speed of 180 km/h (112 mph).

The baseball home plate is 17 inches wide.

Golf is the only sport to have been played on the moon. On 6 February 1971 Alan Shepard hit a golf ball.

Bill Klem served the most seasons as Major League umpire – 37 years, starting in 1905. He also officiated in 18 World Series.

The oldest continuous trophy in sports is the America's Cup. It started in 1851, with Americans winning for a straight 132 years until Australia took the Cup in 1983.

Volleyball was invented by William George Morgan of Holyoke, Massachusetts in 1895.

Ferenc Szisz from Romania, driving a Renault, won the first Formula One Grand Prix held at Le Mans, France in 1906.

Basketball was invented in 1891, by James Naismith, a physical education instructor, who was thinking about new ways of providing exercise for young men. He nailed peach baskets onto the balconies at either end of a gymnasium and challenged his student to throw a soccer ball into them from below. Thus modern basketball was born.

The strongest man in the world is Jouko Ahola of Finland, who holds the record for lifting the heaviest stone in the World Strongman competition. The stone weighed 215 kg (414 lb). The 1,85 m (6 ft) tall Jouko is also the world's car-carrying champion.

Jan Suffolk Todd of the US is considered the world's strongest woman. She was the first woman to lift 1 000 pounds in three power lifts.

The record for the most Major League Baseball career innings is held by Cy Young, with 7 356 innings.

Answers to GENERAL SPORTS TRIVIA on page 28

1. The Strahov Stadium in Prague, Czech Republic, which can accommodate 240 000 spectators; **2.** The Dubai World Cup Race has a prize purse of $4 million; **3.** Roger Bannister; **4.** One fight; **5.** Lottie Dod at the age of 15 years and 285 days; **6.** In Ladies singles; **7.** Wimbledon; **8.** Politics; **9.** Grete Weitz of Norway; **10.** Water polo; **11.** Korfball; **12.** Larry Holmes; **13.** Three; **14.** Chicago; **15.** 92

Justplain Darren & Friends Profile
Ray White

Favourite personal sporting memory?	Apart from the 1995 Rugby World Cup, beating Justplain on the squash court in front of an audience in Bloemfontein. The loser had to wear a dress at a live broadcast. We told Baldrick it was a draw and he had to wear the dress instead. Don't tell him …
What's your idea of a perfect weekend?	Anywhere where my wife wears her bikini – yeah baby …
What would be the best way for a fan to approach you in a bar?	Half naked if my wife isn't looking. If it's a guy, a cold Castle will do … just kidding
What do you refuse to pay for?	Nothing. Why should I get any special treatment?
Tell us a secret of your trade?	Taking the mickey out of Justplain. It takes attention away from any mistakes I may make in the news …
Have you ever been arrested? And for what?	When I was 16 I was stopped by a cop who didn't believe I had a learner's licence. He gave me a hard time so I told him to F-off. It's amazing how brave you feel with a few beers in your belly. He arrested me and I spent the day in jail. I confirmed that day that Boksburg cops have no sense of humour
What's been the lowest task/job you've ever had to perform?	Apart from buying Justplain coffee … let's see … I had to seat customers at a Wimpy with a broad smile on my face. I felt like a bit of a chop
What will always be in your fridge?	Black Labels and my daughter's chocolate milkshake bottles
Favourite 'junk food' meal?	Ribs. The messier the better
What's the last drink you have before going to bed at night?	Milk and cookies of course

What's your biggest indulgence?	Consuming large amounts of alcohol at Rhapsody's. I swear that when I look at Darren, sometimes I see double
Best advice given to you by your mother?	Never try to comb you hair forward to conceal your bald spot. Accept baldness like a man, and don't join others who won't admit to it
What would your profession be if you were not a radio presenter?	I'm a journalist down to the bone. However, I've always wanted to be a fireman and have a Dalmatian
There are Seven Wonders of the World, what's your eighth?	Every time I hear a new hit song on the radio. It's like medicine and seems to put the funk back into me
Your Top 5 list of music?	U2 – One Queen – Bohemian Rhapsody Duran Duran – Wild Boys U2 – Pride Thompson Twins – Hold Me Now
Best 'chirp' you have heard during a sports event?	Hugh Bladen commentating on an All Blacks/Springbok game: 'The man in black has it, yes, it's definitely the man in black …'
Who is your mentor/hero?	My father – the guy knows his stuff
If you could swap places with anyone for a day who would it be, and why?	My one-year-old daughter. She has an absolute party
A quote or phrase that has had an impact on your life or best describes you?	'When all is crumbling around you: just smile.' – Charlie Chaplin
A one-liner that best describes Darren and his radio show?	One helluva party that lasts for four hours daily and sometimes even lands up with you having a hangover the day after

Sports Report *by Baldrick*

This is a report on the 2002 World Cup that John Walland read on 5fm. It was a scam, of course, and had everyone in stitches!

> South Korean coach Guus Hiddink shocked home fans by axing goal scorer Jong Chi Ahn from his team for their World Cup quarter-final against Spain this weekend. Ahn scored the winning golden goal in yesterday's thriller against Italy, and is one of five changes to the side for their crucial match against third favourites Spain. Coming in for Ahn is Fung Kee Song, who hasn't played a game in the tournament yet. Other World Cup debutants include Chee Lik Dong, midfielder Wun Tuu Peh, defenders Yo Gee Sip and Chee Chan Chong, whilst reserve goalkeeper Suk Mi Wang is on standby for goalkeeper Mi Dik Long.

News Booboos *by Ray White*

The listener has the luxury of sitting back and listening to the news, which should be crystal clear and easy to listen to. Little does he or she know what goes on behind the scenes and what near-calamities happen on air.

A newsreader should receive the bulletin at least ten minutes before going on air so that any mistakes can be fixed up. However, sometimes the bulletin is read cold and the newsreader is not as wide awake as he or she should be.

Very often a mistake or a mispronounced word will leave us in total stitches. I cringe when Darren looks my way during a news bulletin and smiles. Two minutes later I usually pay the penalty for my blunder.

One of the funniest mistakes was made by a member of the drive team a few years ago. Without mentioning any names, the person read out that a woman had given birth to a live faeces. He carried on, oblivious to the fact that 'foetus' would have been more appropriate.

Some other gems I've heard or received in my bulletins ...

- The Cape to Ten Rand Yacht Race (not Cape to Rio)
- A person has been trampled to death by a train
- The soldiers left the passing out parade (not pass out)
- The Faah-Cup, not the FA Cup
- There's a Ferrari in Parliament (not a furore)
- Two men entered the store, armed with handguns and a woman
- The leopard was shot on the spot
- The man defecated to the West (not defected)
- Residents of Bryanston are using razor wire as a detergent (not deterrent)
- The son left his mother cooking on the stove before the fire broke out (not at the stove)
- Strikers are thrashing the streets (not trashing)

So as you can see, it's better to pre-read your bulletins so as not to make a total tart of yourself. The public doesn't know that you didn't write the news. In any event, it is your responsibility.

Justplain Darren & Friends Profile
Leigh-Ann Mol

Favourite personal sporting memory?	I've never been the athletic type … So possibly the ONLY sporting memory I have is signing up to run the 400 m at a RAU event, and coming to a halt after about 100 m with an asthma attack
What's your idea of a perfect weekend?	Going away to a game farm with family or friends. There's nothing better than stretching your weekend days to the limit – getting up early to spot game and ending the day with a meal and a quiet chat around a big fire
What would be the best way for a fan to approach you in a bar?	By NOT starting with the line 'Hey, aren't you that chick …' The best for me is striking up a conversation with someone, having an absolute blast, and only at a later stage, they realise who I am. That way, they got to know me as ME first!
What do you refuse to pay for?	I'm a bit of a goodie-two-shoes when it comes to paying for things, but I don't like giving a good tip for bad service
Tell us a secret of your trade?	I'm always myself – that way I don't have to tire myself out by portraying a different personality
Have you ever been arrested? And for what?	No! Like I said, goodie-two-shoes is my middle name …
What's been the lowest task/job you've ever had to perform?	Cleaning toilets during detention for arriving late at school
What will always be in your fridge?	Cheese and mince
Favourite 'junk food' meal?	Artichoke and olive pizza
What's the last drink you have before going to bed at night?	Either alcohol or water – depending on what time I need to be up for work the next day!
What's your biggest indulgence?	Chocolate
Best advice given to you by your mother?	Never try to find Mr Right – he will find you

What would your profession be if you were not a radio presenter?	I would run my own home for abandoned or abused animals
There are Seven Wonders of the World, what's your eighth?	A full body massage, preferably accompanied by an Indian head massage
Your Top 5 list of music?	1. I have a soft spot for live and loud SA music (like the good ol' Springbok Nude Girls and Tree) 2. House and Trance tunes 3. Punk rock (especially the Pixies) 4. 70s classic ballads by bands like Bread, Creedence Clearwater Revival, Chicago and Spandau Ballet 5. 80s–90s sing-along rock tunes (especially Counting Crows)
Best 'chirp' you have heard during a sports event?	I've got two – and they're both from Formula One commentators. The one is: '… and he takes the corner, making it look easy peasy chocolate squeezy …' (I think it was James Allen commentating at the time). The other is a Murray Walker special: '… and Jordan are down, down, down … (long pause) … In the dumps, dumps, dumps.'
Who is your mentor/hero?	I draw my inspiration and knowledge from a number of people, who include my husband, my mom, dad and brother, and of course Michael Schumacher
If you could swap places with anyone for a day who would it be, and why?	A vet who's had a really satisfying day at work. It must feel really good to help those in pain who couldn't tell you so in the first place
A quote or phrase that has had an impact on your life or best describes you?	'If it doesn't happen, it wasn't meant to be.'
A one-liner that best describes Darren and his radio show?	Part of my one-liner would have to include the phrase coined by my dad during his speech at my wedding: 'I see Justplain's show as a challenge for me to withstand the tyranny of the rogues in the afternoon.'

Tyranny of Rogues Tour

Leigh-Ann Mol's Tyranny of Rogues, Once was Virgin, Garter Tour!

Leigh-Ann Mol (née Van der Stadt) ... you know, the dyslexic one on the news and traciff, uh, traffic in the afternoons, finally tied the knot early in 2002. I had heard about a glass that Britney Spears had used on her German Tour to drink water in her hotel room. A German radio DJ got hold of this glass and sent it on tour around Germany, and it became the most famous glass in European history!

I had a cunning plan!

Leigh-Ann would relinquish her garter (or we would beat it out of anyone who caught it at the wedding) and send it on tour ... AROUND THE WORLD, nogal! By the time we had got the garter, the requests to take it to different exotic (and erotic) places had come flooding in! Up to now, the file of e-mail requests is so thick, it must be the thickest file in the history of filing!

The idea is to send the garter with travelling South Africans to world landmarks, sights, events – you name it! The folks who take the garter must photograph the garter at these sights or events, and we put the pics on the website (5fm.co.za – Tyranny of Rogues Tour) for all to follow its progress. The suggestion was also made, and this we are going to do – to have it entered into the Guinness Book of Records as the garter to have travelled more than any other.

The target is to send it to as many parts of the world as it takes to represent each letter of the alphabet (i.e. the A–Z of places). So far it has been to:

- THE BRAZILIAN GRAND PRIX
- THE CAPE ARGUS TOUR (ON A CYCLIST'S LEG)
- THE COMRADES (ON THE ARM OF A SILVER MEDALLIST)

- PORTUGAL
- STAR CITY, KAZAKHSTAN, WITH THE SHUTTLEWORTH TEAM
- RUNNING WITH THE BULLS IN PAMPLONA (WITH NEIL MCKENZIE AND KERRY MACGREGOR)
- AT THE JUSTPLAIN GOLF DAY ON THE 'CLOSEST TO THE GARTER' HOLE
- THE GREAT WALL OF CHINA
- PATPONG ROAD (BANGKOK'S RED LIGHT DISTRICT), THAILAND
- SUNSET STRIP, LAS VEGAS

And is on its way to:

- LONDON WITH THE BOKS IN NOVEMBER
- DOWN A GOLDMINE
- UP KILIMANJARO AND ACONCAGUA
- POLAND
- THROUGH AFRICA
- MADAGASCAR
- ON CONCORDE

Plus many other places ... You can keep track on the website, or on the show, and look out for Tour T-shirts with all the dates and venues when the tour ends in February next year where it started ... in Brazil at the Rio Carnival!

Justplain Darren & Friends Profile
Ashraf Garda

Favourite personal sporting memory?	Watching Dynamos beat Cape Town Spurs 2–0 in the Old Federation Benson & Hedges Cup Final in Durban – in the 1970s
What's your idea of a perfect weekend?	Victory for the SA cricketers/Springboks/Bafana Bafana. My son Zaahid scoring a try and a goal for his respective rugby and soccer teams. Getting to interview the match winners
What would be the best way for a fan to approach you in a bar?	To throw me out! Being Muslim you shouldn't find me there
What do you refuse to pay for?	I will not pay any cricketer to 'underperform' or for any pitch or weather info
Tell us a secret of your trade?	Become friendly with Darren Scott. Oh, and read a lot aloud
Have you ever been arrested? And for what?	In 1979 – for attending a social protest in solidarity with the 16 June uprising. I spent about 10 hours at Protea Police Station
What's been the lowest task/job you've ever had to perform?	Picking up a ball from the net and collecting a ball from under a car while fielding for street a cricket team
What will always be in your fridge?	Something frozen!
Favourite 'junk food' meal?	A toasted steak with cheese
What's the last drink you have before going to bed at night?	I'm a hot chocolate or coffee fanatic

What's your biggest indulgence?	Magazines, books and lots of stationery
Best advice given to you by your mother?	'Don't forget to take your handkerchief to school.' Sadly, I don't use it for 'snotty' things, but to wipe away the tears when my team loses
What would your profession be if you were not a professional radio presenter?	Well, I was in the fashion fabric business, but I suppose it would have to be a frustrated wannabe sportscaster
There are Seven Wonders of the World, what's your eighth?	My late father Sam, who died in July 2002. He taught me good manners, introduced me to reading and encouraged my love of sport
Your Top 5 list of music?	We Are the Champions Lady, by Kenny Rogers Woman in Love In the Air Tonight And a host of Islamic-inspired sounds!
Best 'chirp' you have heard during a sports event?	Being a pretty useless cricketer, it has to be the 'Quack quack' sounds when I'm out for a duck!
Who is your mentor/hero?	I've always admired boxing legend Muhammad Ali
If you could swap places with anyone for a day who would it be, and why?	It would have to be my son Zaahid – he's given me so much joy watching him play sport – and do it well!
A quote or phrase that has had an impact on your life or best describes you?	(1) The sky is not the limit. (2) I've come back from being 2–0 down in the game of life, to lead 3–2. I'd like to wrap it up 5–2.
A one-liner that best describes Darren and his radio show?	A true member of the SA Sports Supporters Club

Sports Gear & Equipment Trivia

1. On a dartboard, what number is directly opposite No. 1?
2. What colour is the cue ball in pool?
3. What is the craft of making arrows called?
4. In cycle racing, what is a sag wagon?
5. The apparatus used by male gymnasts consists of the vaulting horse, pommel horse, horizontal bars, rings and floor. Which of these pieces of apparatus do women use?
6. Essential equipment for a boxer comprises gloves, hand tape, protector below the waist, boots and what else?
7. Why do American footballers paint black marks across their cheeks?
8. In ice hockey what are puck-stoppers?
9. In the early days of cricket, a bowler who took three wickets in a row was presented with a top hat. What modern term comes from this practice?
10. What sport has four different colour codes for the balls, ranging from yellow for hot conditions to blue for cold conditions?
11. Apart from body padding, what protection do baseball players wear?
12. In hot-air ballooning, how is the manoeuvring or cooling valve used?
13. How many red balls are there in snooker?
14. Which sport uses stones and a house?
15. Starting blocks are used on athletic tracks. Runners push their feet against them to get the fastest possible start. What else can they be used for?

16. In fencing, which is the heavier weapon: the foil or the épée?
17. Kendo is one of the traditional Japanese martial arts and the participants use a type of sword. From what is the sword made?
18. What type of shots are woods used for in golf?
19. What colour is the centre scoring zone of an archery target?
20. All the hoops in croquet are painted white, except the last one, called the rover, which has a different colour on the crown. Which colour is it?
21. Why are the officials in American football known as zebras?
22. From what fairly lightweight wood is a cricket bat traditionally made?
23. In archery, what material are the arrows usually made from?
24. Soccer boots have interchangeable studs. The studs for wet and slippery surfaces are made from aluminium. What studs are used for playing on hard ground?

25 How many points is the blue ball worth in snooker?

Answers to SPORTS GEAR & EQUIPMENT TRIVIA on page 49

Justplain Darren & Friends Profile
Corné Krige

Favourite personal sporting memory?	The Currie Cup Finals in 2000 and 2001
What's your idea of a perfect weekend?	In the bush with my wife and lots of wild animals
What would be the best way for a fan to approach you in a bar?	Any way, as long as they are not rude
What do you refuse to pay for?	Sex
Tell us a secret of your trade?	To have a tough mind and be a good key man
Have you ever been arrested? And for what?	Yes, for stealing strawberries at night, while I was at school
What's been the lowest task/job you've ever had to perform?	Driving a forklift in a scrapyard. The forklift had no roof and it was the middle of summer
What will always be in your fridge?	Milk
Favourite 'junk food' meal?	Pizza
What's the last drink you have before going to bed at night?	A protein shake
What's your biggest indulgence?	Jelly sweets
Best advice given to you by your mother?	Always remain humble

What would your profession be if you were not a professional sportsman?	A professional hunter
There are Seven Wonders of the World, what's your eighth?	To manage to find the kind of wife that I have
Your Top 5 list of music?	U2 Matchbox 20 Henry Ate Eagles Paul Simon – Graceland
Best 'chirp' you have heard during a sports event?	I have two: Glenn McGrath asked David Houghton why he was so fat. When the question was asked a second time, David answered: because every time I sleep with your mom she gives me a cookie. The second one is when Dan van Zyl was playing scrumhalf for WP. At that time he had a car sponsor. Upon putting the ball in the scrum he called out his car sponsor's name, hoping to get a bit of advertising on TV
Who is your mentor/hero?	I have none
If you could swap places with anyone for a day who would it be, and why?	Mother Theresa – I want to see what it's really like to give and not to receive anything in return. To also have no expectations
A quote or phrase that has had an impact on your life or best describes you?	'It's not the people with the most awards, most money or most credentials that make a difference in life. It's the people who care.'
A one-liner that best describes Darren and his radio show?	Bizarre!!

Justplain Darren & Friends Profile
Bob Skinstad

Favourite personal sporting memory?	Hong Kong Sevens
What's your idea of a perfect weekend?	Beach, water and friends
What would be the best way for a fan to approach you in a bar?	Friendly 'Hi, howzit going!'
What do you refuse to pay for?	Friends
Tell us a secret of your trade?	Some of the guys are quite superstitious
Have you ever been arrested? And for what?	No
What's been the lowest task/job you've ever had to perform?	Cleaning beer and vomit off the floor when I worked as a barman
What will always be in your fridge?	Cheese and Guinness
Favourite 'junk food' meal?	KFC
What's the last drink you have before going to bed at night?	Horlicks
What's your biggest indulgence?	Chocolate
Best advice given to you by your mother?	Be nice and mean it!

What would your profession be if you were not a professional sportsman?	Advertising/Marketing
There are Seven Wonders of the World, what's your eighth?	Nelson Mandela
Your Top 5 list of music?	1. Bruce Springsteen 2. Del Amitri 3. Pretenders 4. Paul Simon 5. Irish Pub Songs
Best 'chirp' you have heard during a sports event?	**Cricket commentary:** **One commentator said:** 'I think Steve Waugh is the best all-rounder in the world!' **To which the other commentator replied:** 'I don't even think he's the best all-rounder in his family!'
Who is your mentor/hero?	Eclectic: Try to draw from as many people as possible
If you could swap places with anyone for a day who would it be, and why?	Zinedine Zidane – so I could play in the Soccer World Cup
A quote or phrase that has had an impact on your life or best describes you?	'Never let the success of yesterday lull you into the complacency of today, for that is the great foundation of failure.' – O.G. Mandino
A one-liner that best describes Darren and his radio show?	Positive and informative – but still a lot of fun!

Rugby Trivia

1. Who is known as the founder of rugby?
2. In which year was rugby founded?
3. Where is the oldest rugby club in the world?
4. Which rugby club is the oldest in Cape Town?
5. How many players formed an English rugby team in 1871?
6. Who was the first South African rugby captain?
7. Which was the first overseas team to visit South Africa?
8. Which Springbok team was the first to fly overseas?
9. Who scored the first try against an overseas team?
10. Who was the last player to score a three-point try?
11. Who scored the last four-point try?
12. Who scored the first five-point try and in which year?
13. Who was the first Springbok to be replaced in a Test match?
14. Which Springbok rugby captain was awarded an MBE?
15. Which lock played for South Africa in 1984 and then played for the Springboks again after a lapse of nine years?
16. Who was the 500th capped Springbok?
17. Which Springbok held the 400 metres record in athletics?
18. Which player represented both South Africa and Ireland?
19. Which Springbok's brother played for Scotland?
20. Which player refused to wear his Springbok blazer?
21. Who 'invented' the dive pass?

22. Who is the most capped international captain?

23. What is Michael Jones's nickname?

24. Which player played in three different positions for the Springboks from 1960 to 1965?

25. For which two countries did Christian Stewart play?

26. Who was the first Springbok to be sent off the field in a Test?

27. Which three Springboks played in the most World Cup matches?

28. Who won the most Test matches as captain of South Africa?

29. What were 'Kitch' Christie's real given names?

30. Which South African fullback was born in Namibia?

Answers to RUGBY TRIVIA on page 53

Answers to SPORTS GEAR & EQUIPMENT TRIVIA on page 42

1. No. 19; **2.** White; **3.** Fletching; **4.** One of the last vehicles following road events and picking up riders who have dropped out; **5.** Vaulting horse and floor; **6.** Gumshield; **7.** It helps to protect against the sun's glare; **8.** Pads protecting knees and shins; **9.** Hat-trick; **10.** Squash; **11.** Helmet and face mask; **12.** To release hot air for descent; **13.** Fifteen; **14.** Curling; **15.** To detect false starts; **16.** The épée; **17.** Strips of bamboo; **18.** Long shots; **19.** Gold; **20.** Red; **21.** They wear striped shirts; **22.** Willow; **23.** Tubular aluminium alloy; **24.** Rubber studs; **25.** Five

Justplain Darren & Friends Profile
Robbie Fleck

Favourite personal sporting memory?	– 1999 Rugby World Cup – First Test Cap
What's your idea of a perfect weekend?	Beach, sun, surf and fishing with mates ended off with cocktails!
What would be the best way for a fan to approach you in a bar?	Yo Fleckie – how's the injury? … NOT!
What do you refuse to pay for?	Sex … Sometimes!
Tell us a secret of your trade?	Don't give up
Have you ever been arrested? And for what?	Nearly – for dam sliding naked in Cape Town
What's been the lowest task/job you've ever had to perform?	Trainspotter
What will always be in your fridge?	The light!
Favourite 'junk food' meal?	Pizza
What's the last drink you have before going to bed at night?	Chocolate milk … don't forget the bunny!
What's your biggest indulgence?	Eating out

Best advice given to you by your mother?	Shut up!
What would your profession be if you were not a professional sportsman?	Don't have a clue
There are Seven Wonders of the World, what's your eighth?	Cape Town
Your Top 5 list of music?	Red Hot Chili Peppers Travis Coldplay Credence
Best 'chirp' you have heard during a sports event?	The one about the cookies
Who is your mentor/hero?	N/A
If you could swap places with anyone for a day who would it be, and why?	Michael Schumacher
A quote or phrase that has had an impact on your life or best describes you?	N/A
A one-liner that best describes Darren and his radio show?	A laugh

A Springbok supporter landed at Heathrow and, feeling a little unwell, decided to see a doctor.

'Hey, Doc man, I don't feel so good, eh?' he said. The doctor gave him a thorough examination and informed him that he had a serious condition and that the only cure was testicular removal.

'Nooit, Doc,' replied the Sarf Efrican. 'I'm getting a second opinion, my mate!'

The second English doctor gave him the same diagnosis and also advised him that testicular removal was the only cure. Not surprisingly, he refused treatment.

He was devastated. With only hours before the Boks' opening game he found an ex-pat South African doctor and decided to get a final opinion from someone he could trust. The doctor examined him and said, 'Sorry, boet, you's very siek, eh!'

'What's the cure then, Doc?' he asked, hoping for a different answer.

'Ons moet jou ballas afsny, ou maat.'

'Pragtig, thenk you for thet,' he said. 'Those rooinek bastards wanted to take my test tickets off me!'

A South African is drinking in a New York bar when his cellphone rings. He hangs up grinning from ear to ear and orders a round for the whole bar, announcing that his wife just gave birth to a 12 kg baby boy. Nobody can believe the weight, but the South African just shrugs and says, 'We make 'em big back home, folks. My boy is typically South African.' Congratulations are showered on him and many exclamations of 'Wow!' are heard. One woman even faints due to sympathy pains.

Two weeks later the South African returns to the same bar. The barman says, 'We were going to call you. Everyone's been making bets as to how much your 12 kg son weighs now. Sooooooooo, how much does he weigh now?'

The proud father answers that he now weighs 10.5 kg.

The barman is puzzled and concerned, and asks: 'What happened? He already weighed 12 kg on the day he was born!'

The South African father takes a slow swig from his long-neck Castle beer, wipes his lips on his khaki shirt, leans proudly over to the bartender and says, 'Had him circumcised, boet.'

Schools Rugby

Here are the standings at the end of 2001:

1. Affies
2. Grey College
3. Boland Landbou
4. Grey High School
5. Maritzburg College
6. HTS Middelburg
7. PW Botha
8. Daniël Pienaar
9. Monument
10. Outeniqua
11. Paarl Boys' High
12. Oakdale
13. Kearsney
14. DHS
15. Paarl Gim
16. Klerksdorp
17. Pretoria Boys' High
18. Die Brandwag
19. Waterkloof
20. St Andrew's

Answers to RUGBY TRIVIA on page 48

1. William Webb Ellis; **2.** 1823; **3.** Guys Hospital Rugby side, founded in 1864; **4.** Hamiltons founded in 1875; **5.** Twenty players; **6.** H.H. Castens; **7.** W.E. MacLagan's side from Britain; **8.** Basie Viviers' 1956 team to New Zealand; **9.** Hasie Versfeld in 1891; **10.** Pieter Cronjé in 1971; **11.** Johan Heunis in 1989; **12.** Danie Gerber in 1992; **13.** Dawie de Villiers; **14.** Des van Jaarsveld; **15.** Vleis Visagie; **16.** Willie du Plessis; **17.** Jaco Reinach; **18.** Jack Gage; **19.** Dugald McDonald; **20.** Faan Conradie from South Western Districts; **21.** Daunce Divine; **22.** Will Carling (England), 54 times; **23.** 'Iceberg'; **24.** Dave Stewart; **25.** Canada and South Africa; **26.** James Small; **27.** Joost van der Westhuizen, Mark Andrews and Os du Randt; **28.** Gary Teichman, with 36 matches; **29.** George Moir; **30.** Percy Montgomery, born in Walvis Bay

Justplain Darren & Friends Profile
Rob Kempson

Favourite personal sporting memory?	Beating Selbourne UISA 1876. They were unbeaten at the time and had beaten us 34-0 the previous game. Thanks Avos
What's your idea of a perfect weekend?	Anywhere away, friends, your average barbeque and Cypress Hill
What would be the best way for a fan to approach you in a bar?	Any way without attitude or your normal Dutch arrogance
What do you refuse to pay for?	Any event that SARFU organises
Tell us a secret of your trade?	I keep people busy on my and not on the ball
Have you ever been arrested? And for what?	N/A
What's been the lowest task/job you've ever had to perform?	Being a barman
What will always be in your fridge?	Champagne – Moët, Pongracz or Steenberg
Favourite 'junk food' meal?	Chrunchie (biscuit) and milk/Oros
What's the last drink you have before going to bed at night?	Water or wine
What's your biggest indulgence?	Any night out!

Best advice given to you by your mother?	Always remember the little guy!
What would your profession be if you were not a professional sportsman?	Lawyer
There are Seven Wonders of the World, what's your eighth?	Perhaps your above average female!
Your Top 5 list of music?	Fat Boy Slim Live – Lightning Crashes Verdi Nickleback Cat Stevens – Father and Son
Best 'chirp' you have heard during a sports event?	Fleckie booing Manny Edmonds after he fluffed a drop-goal
Who is your mentor/hero?	Gary Teichmann
If you could swap places with anyone for a day who would it be, and why?	Monty – just for that perfect evening with Tasmin
A quote or phrase that has had an impact on your life or best describes you?	'How far you go in life depends on your being tender with the young, compassionate with the aged, sympathetic with the striving and tolerant of the weak and the strong. Because someday in life, you would have been all of these.'
A one-liner that best describes Darren and his radio show?	Darren Twat and the Hill-Billies

Justplain Darren & Friends Profile
Joel Stransky

Favourite personal sporting memory?	I count myself fortunate to have many great memories, but naturally the one that stands out is the 1995 Rugby World Cup final. From Mr Mandela coming into the change room to wish us luck to the final whistle, and including the drop, it was just a special day.
What's your idea of a perfect weekend?	A bit different here in Johannesburg. When I lived at the sea, it was time on our fishing boat and a crayfish braai. And maybe some golf. Here in Johannesburg it would be a round of golf, a decent ride on my bike and time with my family and friends.
What would be the best way for a fan to approach you in a bar?	In a friendly manner. I struggle to hide my irritation at those who run you down, try to make you look bad or just know everything. I like chatting to honestly friendly people and there are lots of them!
What do you refuse to pay for?	Poor service!
Tell us a secret of your trade?	Self-belief and confidence! If you don't believe you are the best, you never will be!
Have you ever been arrested? And for what?	Sadly, the answer is yes, for disturbing the peace. It was a 'digs' party at Rudolf Straeuli's (yes, our coach) commune and when the police arrived for the third time, everyboby ran out of a secret hole in the back fence into a park. Only problem was that three of us did not know where the hole was and had no escape route. Rudolf did try in vain to get us released immediately, but probably just made it worse!
What's been the lowest task/job you've ever had to perform?	While in the Air Force I had to pick up 'stompies' along the Air Force Base's road. Horrible! Fortunately I never had to clean the toilets!
What will always be in your fridge?	Chocolate, yoghurt and a few beers!
Favourite 'junk food' meal?	Pizza and a milkshake!
What's the last drink you have before going to bed at night?	Hot chocolate! I actually got in the habit while sharing a room with Mark Andrews during the 1995 World Cup and then on tour. Every night my roommate would make us both hot chocolate or he would order room service. The habit has stuck.

What's your biggest indulgence?	A good few drinks with my mates! And it normally turns into a late night as a result. And I have a sweet tooth – sweets, cake, chocolates ...
Best advice given to you by your mother?	Stay modest and humble. I don't think I always listened but I would like to think that in some way I have listened in the long run, learned from my mistakes and taken the good advice! Although Darren and others will disagree!
What would your profession be if you were not a professional correspondent?	I am only a part-time correspondent and if I weren't I would be coaching part time.
There are Seven Wonders of the World, what's your eighth?	The perfect round of golf. It is obviously not possible as you would still be able to have done something better even if you shot 59! (Not 69, Darren)
Your Top 5 list of music?	U2 Hothouse Flowers Counting Crows Pink Floyd The Calling
Best 'chirp' you have heard during a sports event?	Player asked the ref if he was blind. The ref turned and asked angrily: 'What did you say?' and another player chirped: 'And he's deaf as well!'
Who is your mentor/hero?	I think your father is always one of your mentors and mine is no different. He has been a tower of strength, help and advice. In rugby there have been many great coaches from Kitch Christie to Bob Dwyer and many in the middle. But the one man who I will always consider to be an 'older brother' is HO de Villiers.
If you could swap places with anyone for a day who would it be, and why?	Probably someone who spends his life having lots of fun, and getting paid for it. Someone who goes to exotic places with stunning models to shoot the swimwear calendar for a sports mag. Someone who spends his life talking absolute nonsense for a living. Who could that be?
A quote or phrase that has had an impact on your life or best describes you?	'Be the best you possibly can!' – Bob Dwyer
A one-liner that best describes Darren and his radio show?	Pack your suitcase, you are going on a trip! (Reference to that disgusting drink he makes everyone consume with him!)

Joel's typical night out

Rhapsody's Cafe
Telephone: 463-0977 or 7948
Vat Number: 4790154829

10 Top Sect

Tbl 266/1 Chk 3017 Gst 3
CLOSED
08Aug'02 20:34

Eat In

1	Mineral Still	8.20
2	Red Bull	49.80
3	Lime Cordial	2.70
2	Soda	13.80
1	Coke	6.90
2	Heineken	21.20
1	Savanna	11.60
1	Smirnoff Ice	11.90
3	Jameson	27.60
6	Water Mix	0.00
12	Dbl Jack Daniels	276.00
3	Jack Daniels	34.50
2	Smirnoff Vodka	11.80
1	Dbl Klipdrift	11.80
1	Dbl Smirnoff	11.80
1	Bells	8.00
93	Suitcase	1181.10
	Charge Tip	200.00
	Acct Charge	1888.70
	Subtotal	1688.70
	Service Chrg	200.00
	Payment	1888.70

10 Check Closed
09Aug'02 01:51

Aussie Jokes

Three South Africans and three Australians are travelling by train to a rugby match. At the station, the three Aussies each buy a ticket and watch as the three South Africans buy only a single ticket.

'How are three people going to travel on only one ticket?' asks one of the Aussies.

'Watch and you'll see,' answers one of the South Africans.

They all board the train. The Aussies take their respective seats, but all three South Africans cram into a restroom and close the door behind them. Shortly after the train departs, the conductor comes around collecting tickets. He knocks on the restroom door and says, 'Ticket, please.' The door opens just a crack and a single arm emerges with a ticket in hand. The conductor takes it and moves on.

The Aussies see this and agree it is quite a clever idea. So, after the rugby match they decide to copy the South Africans on the return trip and save some money. When they get to the station, they buy a single ticket for the return trip. To their astonishment, the South Africans don't buy a ticket at all.

'How are you going to travel without a ticket?' asks one perplexed Aussie.

'Watch and you'll see,' says one of the South Africans.

When they board the train, the three Aussies cram into a restroom and the three South Africans cram into another one nearby. The train departs. Shortly afterwards, one of the South Africans leaves the restroom and walks over to the restroom where the Aussies are hiding. He knocks on the door and says, 'Ticket, please.'

A South African is having a quiet drink in a bar. He leans over to the big bloke next to him and says, 'Do you want to hear an Australian joke?'

The big bloke replies, 'Well, mate, before you tell that joke, you should know something. I'm 1.80 m tall, I weigh 105 kg and I played in the forwards for the Wallabies. The guy next to me is 1.95 m, weighs 115 kg and he's an ex-Wallaby lock. Next to him is a bloke who's 2 m tall, weighs 120 kg and he's a current Wallaby second rower. Now do you still want to tell that Australian joke?'

The South African says, 'No way, not if I'm going to have to explain it three times.'

Once, a long time ago, there was a Wallaby tour of New Zealand. During their stay in Wellington, one of the players had a fairly torrid affair with a local lass. The team moved on, the girl stayed behind, and the whole thing was eventually forgotten about.

Four years later, the same player returns to New Zealand with another Wallaby touring side. They are in Wellington, and who should he see walking down the street but his lover with a small child! He runs up to her and greets her, and asks if the child is his. 'Yes,' she says, 'it is.'

'But why didn't you tell me?' he asked plaintively.

'Well,' she said, 'after I found out I was pregnant, I invited all the members of my family together for a discussion on the matter – my grandparents, my parents, my uncles, aunts and cousins. And we all came to the same conclusion: we would rather that it was a bastard than have a Wallaby for a father.'

Ross has been in business for 25 years and is finally sick of the stress.

He quits his job and buys 50 acres in the Outback as far from humanity as possible.

He sees the postman once a week and gets groceries once a month.

Otherwise it's total peace and quiet.

After six months or so of almost total isolation, someone knocks on his door.

He opens it and there stands a big, bearded man.

'Name's Bruce ... your neighbour from 40 miles away ... Having a Christmas party Friday ... thought you might like to come ... about five o'clock ...'

'Great,' says Ross. 'After six months out here I'm ready to meet some local folks. Thank you.'

As Bruce is leaving, he stops. 'Gotta warn you ... there's gonna be some drinkin'.'

'Not a problem ... after 25 years in business, I can drink with the best of 'em.'

Again, as he starts to leave, Bruce stops. 'More 'n likely gonna be some fightin' too.'

Ross says, 'Well, I get along with people. I'll be there. Thanks again.'

Once again Bruce turns from the door. 'I've seen some wild sex at these parties, too.'

'Now that's really not a problem,' says Ross. 'I've been all alone for six months! I'll definitely be there. By the way, what should I bring?'

Bruce stops in the door again and says, 'Whatever you want. Just gonna be the two of us.'

A man walks into a shop and asks to buy half a head of lettuce.

The shop assistant tells him that they only sell whole heads of lettuce, but the customer replies that he does not need a whole head, only a half head. The assistant says he will go and ask his manager about the matter. The boy walks into the back room and says, 'There is some arsehole out there who wants to buy only a half head of lettuce.' As he is finishing saying this he turns around to find the customer standing right behind him, so he adds, 'and this gentleman wants to buy the other half.'

The manager okays the deal and the customer goes on his way. Later the manager calls the boy and says, 'You almost got yourself into a lot of trouble earlier, but I must say I was impressed with the way you got yourself out of it. You think on your feet and we like that around here. Where are you from, son?'

'Australia, sir,' replies the boy.

'You're joking! Why did you leave Australia?' asks the manager.

The boy replies, 'They're all just whores and rugby players over there.'

'My wife is from Australia!' shouts the manager.

'Really!' replies the boy. 'What team did she play for?'

Tough decision

You're relaxing at the beach and see two guys drowning in the sea. One is Australian and the other is a Kiwi. You only have enough time to save one of them.

Do you: (a) carry on reading your paper, or (b) go for lunch?

An Australian man was shipwrecked on a desert island with nobody for company except his faithful sheepdog. Life was getting monotonous until one day he spotted a sheep on the other side of the island. Slowly approaching the sheep, he managed to get it into position and was about to do his thing, when his dog suddenly gave a loud bark and began herding the animal away from its master. All subsequent attempts to approach the sheep were equally frustrated by the dog.

A few months later, a pretty girl was washed ashore and the man frantically resuscitated her. The girl was profusely thankful and offered to do anything for him in return. 'Good!' said the love-struck man happily. 'Can you watch my dog for fifteen minutes?'

An Englishman wanted to become an Irishman, so he visited a doctor to find out how to go about this. 'Well,' said the doctor, 'this is a very delicate operation and there is a lot that can go wrong. I will have to remove half your brain.'

'That's OK,' said the Englishman. 'I've always wanted to be Irish and I'm prepared to take the risk.'

The operation went ahead, but the Englishman woke to find a look of horror on the face of the doctor.

'I'm so terribly sorry!' the doctor said. 'Instead of removing half the brain, I've taken the whole brain out.'

The patient replied, 'No worries, mate!'

Justplain Darren & Friends Profile
Shaun Pollock

Favourite personal sporting memory?	– Playing for South Africa for the first time – South Africa winning the Rugby World Cup
What's your idea of a perfect weekend?	Enjoying good company at home with my wife, friends and family … dinners, braais and managing to fit in a round of golf at some stage
What would be the best way for a fan to approach you in a bar?	Quietly and with minimal fuss
What do you refuse to pay for?	Five years ago I would've said water (and clearly things have changed), so I hope one day I'll never have to pay for clean air
Tell us a secret of your trade?	Disregard reputations and avoid the trap of being dictated to by the opposition
Have you ever been arrested? And for what?	No, not yet!
What's been the lowest task/job you've ever had to perform?	Cleaning up after pets …
What will always be in your fridge?	Milk and strawberry yoghurt
Favourite 'junk food' meal?	McDonalds Quarter Pounder burger, no onions
What's the last drink you have before going to bed at night?	Water (just enough!)
What's your biggest indulgence?	International phone calls and golfing equipment

Best advice given to you by your mother?	Don't swear on the field
What would your profession be if you were not a professional sportsman?	Probably marketing
There are Seven Wonders of the World, what's your eighth?	Tiger Woods
Your Top 5 list of music?	The Whole of the Moon – Waterboys If You're Gone – Matchbox Twenty Two Princes – Spin Doctors Summergirls – LFO With Arms Wide Open – Creed
Best 'chirp' you have heard during a sports event?	Symmo giving Ranatunga stick about losing so much weight despite being sponsored by Sam's Chicken and Ribs
Who is your mentor/hero?	Malcolm Marshall – awesome cricketer who taught me so much
If you could swap places with anyone for a day who would it be, and why?	Head of the Secret Service/CIA because I'd have the authority to find out whether we've been visited by extra-terrestrials yet, who really killed JFK and the answers to other conspiracy theories …
A quote or phrase that has had an impact on your life or best describes you?	'Believe in yourself, because if you don't then who will?'
A one-liner that best describes Darren and his radio show?	Well worth the effort of linking up to streaming audio anywhere in the world!

Cricket Trivia

1. Who was the first cricketer to score a triple century and a century in a Test match?
2. What was South Africa's highest opening stand at the 1999 World Cup?
3. Who scored the highest number of runs per over in the 1996 World Cup?
4. Who captained India at the 1999 World Cup?
5. In which year was the Benson & Hedges series introduced in South African cricket?
6. Which bowler was the first to achieve 100 wickets in Benson & Hedges night series cricket?
7. Who scored the most runs for South Africa at the Commonwealth Games?
8. Who scored the fastest Test century for South Africa in terms of balls faced?
9. Which two South African players have been on the field throughout an entire Test match?
10. What is the highest number of runs scored by a player in four successive games in One Day Internationals?
11. Who was the youngest player to score a double century in first-class cricket in South Africa?
12. Who scored his maiden first-class hundred in a Test match for South Africa, reaching the milestone with a six?
13. Who made the first Currie Cup century?
14. Who was the first player to appear in a first-class cricket match for Barbados and Western Province in the same season?

15. What is the lowest fourth innings target for a team to be set, and still lose the match?
16. Who is the oldest player to have made a Test double century?
17. Who was the youngest player to score a triple century in a Test match?
18. Who scored 256 runs and bowled 97 overs in a Test match?
19. Who is the only batsman to score 1 000 runs in his last year of Test cricket?
20. Who was GS Sobers' first Test wicket?
21. What is the highest wicket partnership at Lords?
22. Who is the only bowler to have taken 15 wickets including a hat trick in the same Test?
23. Which batsman had successive Test innings of 99, 98 and 97?
24. Who is the only wicket-keeper to have taken a hat trick of stumpings off one bowler?
25. Who was the first batsman to score 300 runs in a Test match?
26. What is the lowest score made by a batsman carrying his bat in a first-class cricket match?
27. Who has taken the least number of Tests to reach 50 wickets?
28. Name the batsman who scored 100 before lunch in both innings of a match?
29. Which player, who played a minimum of 50 Test matches, has the best batting average?
30. Who captained South Africa against Australia in 1970?

Answers to CRICKET TRIVIA on page 75

Justplain Darren & Friends Profile
Mike Haysman

Favourite personal sporting memory?	Watching the New York Yankees
What's your idea of a perfect weekend?	Sitting in front of my TV watching Australia win a cricket Test, a rugby Test, watching Kathy Freeman win gold, Ian Thorpe also winning gold, Troy Bayliss destroying his opponents with some light relief from Kylie Minogue, Russell Crowe and Nicole Kidman
What would be the best way for a fan to approach you in a bar?	With a beer in hand
What do you refuse to pay for?	Sex
Tell us a secret of your trade?	Take the piss out of Justplain at every opportunity
Have you ever been arrested? And for what?	As we all know it is a prerequisite for Australians to have a criminal record, so this is a very silly question!
What's been the lowest task/job you've ever had to perform?	Bowling off-spin in first-class cricket and being captained by Justplain in a cricket match
What will always be in your fridge?	Beer
Favourite 'junk food' meal?	Beer
What's the last drink you have before going to bed at night?	Beer
What's your biggest indulgence?	Beer

Best advice given to you by your mother?	Never trust a Kiwi
What would your profession be if you were not a professional correspondent?	A professional correspondent!
There are Seven Wonders of the World, what's your eighth?	Michelle Pfeiffer
Your Top 5 list of music?	Nickleback Jimmy Barnes INXS Anastacia Rolling Stones
Best 'chirp' you have heard during a sports event?	During a recent match in Zimbabwe, a Zimbabwe farmer was facing Glenn McGrath and copping an enormous amount of abuse. Glenn kept calling him a fat @#$%. He replied in no uncertain terms that yes, Glenn was right, but it was due to the fact that every time he gave McGrath's wife one she gave him a biscuit
Who is your mentor/hero?	Darren Schwab
If you could swap places with anyone for a day who would it be, and why?	David E Kelly – he is married to Michelle Pfeiffer
A quote or phrase that has had an impact on your life or best describes you?	Thirsty, very thirsty
A one-liner that best describes Darren and his radio show?	Entertaining organised chaos

Cricket Quotes

'A fart competing with thunder.'
– Graham Gooch summing up England's Ashes attempt in 1990/91

'If the Poms bat first, let's tell the taxi to wait.'
– Banner waved by an Australian during the 1986/87 Ashes series

'Don't swat the flies, Jardine; they're the only friends you've got in Australia.'
– Jeer from Australian fans during the Bodyline series

'If someone had produced a batting helmet during the Bodyline series, I would certainly have worn it.'
– Sir Donald Bradman

'Boycott and controversy have shared the longest opening partnership in the game.'
– Terry Brindle on Geoffrey Boycott

'He spoilt the game – he got too many runs.'
– Sir Jack Hobbs on Sir Donald Bradman

'It's not easy to bat with tears in your eyes.'
– Sir Donald Bradman referring to his last Test innings

'Pitches are like wives; you can never tell how they're going to turn out.'
– Sir Len Hutton referring to cricket pitches

'... and Ray Illingworth is relieving himself in front of the pavilion.'
– John Arlott

'A brain scan revealed that Andrew Caddick is not suffering from stress fracture of the shin.'
– Jo Sheldon

'The Queen's Park Oval, exactly as the name suggests – absolutely round.'
– Tony Crozier

More Aussie Jokes

You might be an Aussie if...

- You've been married three times and still have the same in-laws.
- You wonder how service stations keep their toilets so clean.
- You let your 12-year-old daughter smoke at the dinner table in front of her kids.
- Last year you hid Easter eggs under cow pies.
- Jack Daniels makes your list of 'Most Admired People'.
- You've got more than one brother called Darryl.
- You think that Dom Perignon is a Mafia leader.
- Your wife's hairdo was once ruined by a ceiling fan.
- You take a six-pack to church.
- You go to your family reunion looking for a date.
- You lit a match in the bathroom and your house exploded right off its wheels.

An Afrikaner, an Australian and a West Indian are sitting in the maternity ward of a hospital waiting for the imminent birth of their children.

They are all very nervous and pacing the floor when the doctor bursts through the door and says: 'Congratulations, gentlemen, your wives have all given birth to baby boys within five minutes of each other.'

The men are full of pride and congratulate each other. But then the doctor says: 'However, in all the confusion, we mixed up the babies so we don't know which one belongs to whom. We'd be grateful if you could help us identify them.'

With that, the Afrikaner races past the other two men into the nursery and picks up the dark-skinned baby with dreadlocks, saying: 'There's absolutely no doubt about it. This one's mine!'

The doctor, a little surprised, says: 'But, sir, I would have thought that perhaps this baby is of West Indian descent.'

The Afrikaner replies: 'Well, that may be, but one of the other babies is an Aussie, and I'm not taking the risk!'

A South African ventriloquist visiting Australia walks into a small town and sees a local sitting on his porch patting his dog. He figures he'll have a little fun.

Ventriloquist: 'Howzit, mate, good-looking dog. Mind if I talk to him?

Aussie: 'The dog doesn't talk, you stupid idiot.'

Ventriloquist: 'Hey, dog, howzit going, old mate?'

Dog: 'Doing all right.'

Aussie: [extreme look of shock]

Ventriloquist: 'Is this Aussie your owner?'

Dog: 'Yep.'

Ventriloquist: 'How does he treat you?'

Dog: 'Really good. He walks me twice a day, feeds me great food, and takes me to the lake once a week to play.'

Aussie: [look of disbelief]

Ventriloquist: 'Mind if I talk to your horse?'

Aussie: 'Horse doesn't talk either.'

Ventriloquist: 'Hey, horse, howzit going?'

Horse: 'Cool.'

Aussie: [Extreme look of shock]

Ventriloquist: 'Is this your owner?' [pointing at Aussie]

Horse: 'Yep.'

Ventriloquist: 'How does he treat you?'

Horse: 'Pretty good, thanks for asking. He rides me regularly, brushes me down often, and keeps me in the barn to protect me from the elements.'

Aussie: [total look of amazement]

Ventriloquist: 'Mind if I talk to your sheep?'

Aussie: 'The sheep's a f***ing liar.'

What's the difference between Aussies and pigs?
Pigs don't turn into Aussies when they drink.

What's the difference between an Australian and a computer?
You only have to punch information into a computer once.

Why do birds fly upside down over Australia?
It's not worth shitting on.

Why was the Christ child not born in Australia?
You'd have a job finding three wise men, much less a virgin!!!

What do you call a field full of Australians?
A vacant lot.

How do you define 144 Australians?
Gross stupidity.

The Aussie pilot, when asked for his height and position, replied,
'I'm 5'11 and sitting in the front seat.'

What do you call an Aussie who scores well in an IQ test?
A cheat.

What's the difference between yoghurt and Australians?
At least yoghurt starts with a little culture.

What do you call an Aussie with half a brain?
Gifted.

If Santa Claus, a smart Aussie and a dumb blonde were in a room, and you tossed in a hundred dollar note, who would grab it first?
The blonde – the other two don't exist.

How many Aussies does it take to make chocolate chip cookies?
Ten. One to make the batter, and nine to peel the Smarties.

Did you hear about the Aussie who had a brain transplant?
The brain rejected him a week later.

Answers to CRICKET TRIVIA on page 66

1. Graham Gooch against India; **2.** 176 against New Zealand; **3.** S. Jayasuriya scored 7,94 runs per over; **4.** Mohammad Azharuddin; **5.** 1981/82; **6.** Eric Simons; **7.** Jacques Kallis, 153 runs; **8.** Jonty Rhodes, 103 in 95 balls; **9.** Jackie McGlew and Herschelle Gibbs; **10.** 382 by Gary Kirsten (66 v Kenya, 118 v Pakistan, 84 v India & 105 v Australia); **11.** J Myburgh for Northerns B during the 1997/98 season; **12.** PL Winslow, England v South Africa in 1955; **13.** A Tancred, Kimberley v Transvaal 1889/90 – he scored 106; **14.** EL Challenor 1895/96; **15.** 42, set by Eastern Province for Border to achieve during 1946/47 season; **16.** E Rowan (South Africa) scored 236 in 1951, at the age of 42 years and 7 days; **17.** Gary Sobers (West Indies) at the age of 21 during the 1957/58 season; **18.** MH Mankad (India), England v India, 1952; **19.** DG Bradman who scored 1005 runs in 8 Tests in 1948; **20.** TE Bailey (England); **21.** 424* for the 3rd wicket, between W Edrich and D Compton; **22.** GA Lohmann (England) SA v England, 1895/96; **23.** C Hill during the Australia v England series of 1901/02; **24.** W Bain (Gloucestershire, 1895 off C Townsend); **25.** RE Foster (England) He scored 287 & 19 during the Australia v England games in Sydney, 1903/04; **26.** 5 not out by R Barlow (Lancashire, 1882); **27.** CB Turner (Australia) – 6 Tests; **28.** GL Jessop in 1900 (He scored 104 in the first innings and 139 in the second); **29.** Sir Donald Bradman with an average of 99.94; **30.** Ali Bacher

Justplain Darren & Friends Profile
Lucas Radebe

Favourite personal sporting memory?	I have many favourite sporting memories, but two in particular come to mind: my first game as captain of Bafana Bafana and my first game as captain of Leeds United. Other highlights include Bafana's victory in the 1996 African Cup of Nations on home soil
What's your idea of a perfect weekend?	Leeds playing in the final game of the season at Old Trafford knowing that we have already won the league with Man United coming second. The only thing better than that would be to beat them in that game as well
What would be the best way for a fan to approach you in a bar?	Depends if it is a male or a female …
What do you refuse to pay for?	I generally try to pay for everything – I believe that there is no such thing as a free lunch. If I had to refuse to pay for something, it would probably be a season ticket at Old Trafford. As a Leeds United player, there are certain things that one does and certain things that one doesn't do
Tell us a secret of your trade?	No secrets – just hard work
Have you ever been arrested? And for what?	Not that I remember
What's been the lowest task/job you've ever had to perform?	I cannot recall any tasks that I have not enjoyed but many that I have. The annual Leeds fancy dress evening when the players dress up in theme is always a highlight on my social calendar
What will always be in your fridge?	Chicken
Favourite 'junk food' meal?	CHICKEN
What's the last drink you have before going to bed at night?	Usually water

What's your biggest indulgence?	I have a passion for fast cars, trendy clothes and good music
Best advice given to you by your mother?	That if I work hard I will be rewarded for my efforts, and then I should never forget my roots
What would your profession be if you were not a professional sportsman?	At the time I was signed by Chiefs I was actually studying to become a geography teacher, so I may well have ended up behind a desk or in front of a classroom of kids
There are Seven Wonders of the World, what's your eighth?	This is not a question of what but of who. Nelson Mandela would be my answer without doubt
Your Top 5 list of music?	It would be difficult for me to identify just five different artists or songs. I love relaxing and listening to music. Different music appeals to me at different times. When I am in Leeds I love listening to South African artists such as Jimmy Dludlu. I also listen to lots of soul such as Mary J Blige
Best 'chirp' you have heard during a sports event?	I have been fortunate enough to have played in England with the likes of Vinnie Jones and against the likes of Gazza, and so I have been exposed to great chirps all the time
Who is your mentor/hero?	Nelson Mandela
If you could swap places with anyone for a day who would it be, and why?	The wealthiest man in the world, so that I could donate money to the people of our beautiful country, the children of our Rainbow Nation, who deserve every cent they receive
A quote or phrase that has had an impact on your life or best describes you?	If you can dream it you can do it
A one-liner that best describes Darren and his radio show?	A full game of exciting end-to end football

Football Quotes

'Alex Ferguson is the best manager I've ever had at this level. Well, he's the only manager I've actually had at this level. But he's the best manager I've ever had.'

– David Beckham

'I would not be bothered if we lost every game as long as we won the league.'

– Mark Viduka

'My parents have been there for me, ever since I was about seven.'

– David Beckham

'If you don't believe you can win, there is no point in getting out of bed at the end of the day.'

– Neville Southall

'I've had 14 bookings this season – 8 of which were my fault, but 7 of which were disputable.'

– Paul Gascoigne

'I've never wanted to leave. I'm here for the rest of my life, and hopefully after that as well.'

– Alan Shearer

'I'd like to play for an Italian club, like Barcelona.'

– Mark Draper

'You've got to believe that you're going to win, and I believe we'll win the World Cup until the final whistle blows and we're knocked out.'

– Peter Shilton

'I was watching the Blackburn game on TV on Sunday when it flashed on the screen that George (Ndah) had scored in the first minute at Birmingham. My first reaction was to ring him up. Then I remembered he was out there playing.'

– Ade Akinbiyi

'Without being too harsh on David Beckham, he cost us the match.'

– Ian Wright

'I'm as happy as I can be – but I have been happier.'
– Ugo Ehiogu

'Leeds is a great club and it's been my home for years, even though I live in Middlesborough.'
– Jonathan Woodgate

'I can see the carrot at the end of the tunnel.'
– Stuart Pearce

'I took a whack on my left ankle, but something told me it was my right.'
– Lee Hendrie

'I couldn't settle in Italy – it was like living in a foreign country.'
– Ian Rush

'Germany are a very difficult team to play … they had 11 internationals out there today.'
– Steve Lomas

'I always used to put my right boot on first, and then obviously my right sock.'
– Barry Venison

'I definitely want Brooklyn to be christened, but I don't know into what religion yet.'
– David Beckham

'The Brazilians were South American, and the Ukrainians will be more European.'
– Phil Neville

'All that remains is for a few dots and commas to be crossed.'
– Mitchell Thomas

'One accusation you can't throw at me is that I've always done my best.'
– Alan Shearer

'I'd rather play in front of a full house than an empty crowd.'
– Johnny Giles

'Sometimes in football you have to score goals.'
– Thierry Henry

'I was surprised, but I always say nothing surprises me in football.'
– Les Ferdinand

'It was like the ref had a brand new yellow card and wanted to see if it worked.'
– Richard Rufus

'There's no in between – you're either good or bad. We were in between.'
– Gary Lineker

'Winning doesn't really matter as long as you win.'
– Vinny Jones

'If you don't concede any goals you'll win more games than you lose.'
– Wayne Bridge

'Two Andy Gorams, there's only two Andy Gorams ...'
– Kilmarnock fans to the Rangers keeper after he had been diagnosed with mild schizophrenia

'I've told the players we need to win so I can have the cash to buy some new ones.'
– Chris Turner, Peterborough manager, before LC QF, 1992

'Tell the Kraut to get his ass up front. We don't pay a million for a guy to hang around in defence.'
– NY Cosmos executive on Beckenbauer's positioning

'I spent a lot of my money on booze, birds and fast cars. The rest I just squandered.'
– George Best

'If we played like that every week we wouldn't be so inconsistent.'
– Bryan Robson, Man U, 1990

'That's great, tell him he's Pele and get him back on.'
– John Lambie, Partick Thistle manager, when told a concussed striker did not know who he was

'I was saying the other day, how often the most vulnerable area for goalies is between their legs ...'
– Andy Gray, Sky Sports

Richard Keys 'Well Roy, do you think that you'll have to finish above Manchester United to win the League?

Roy Evans 'You have to finish above everyone to win the league, Richard.'

'If you can't stand the heat in the dressing-room, get out of the kitchen.'
– Terry Venables, Capital Gold

'Football today, it's a game of chess. It's all about money.'
– Newcastle United fan, Radio 5 Live

'I'm not a believer in luck … but I do believe you need it.'
– Alan Ball

'Merseyside derbies usually last 90 minutes and I'm sure today's won't be any different.'
– Trevor Brooking

'Dumbarton player Steve McCahill has limped off with a badly cut forehead.'
– Tom Ferrie

'And I honestly believe we can go all the way to Wembley … unless somebody knocks us out.'
– Dave Basett

'And Arsenal now have plenty of time to dictate the last few seconds.'
– Peter Jones

'What makes this game so delightful is that when both teams get the ball they are attacking their opponent's goal.'
– Jimmy Hill

'Newcastle, of course, unbeaten in their last five wins.'
– Brian Moore

'Strangely, in slow motion replay, the ball seemed to hang in the air for even longer.'
– David Acfield

'What I said to them at half-time would be unprintable on the radio.'
– Gerry Francis

'John Harkes going to Sheffield, Wednesday.'
– New York Post, 1993

‘If there weren’t such a thing as football, we’d all be frustrated footballers.’
– Mick Lyons

‘He’s one of those footballers whose brains are in his head.’
– Derek Johnstone, BBC TV Scotland

‘The crown think that Todd handled the ball ... they must have seen something that nobody else did.’
– Barry Davies, 1975

Jimmy Hill ‘Don’t sit on the fence Terry, what chance do you think Germany has got of getting through?’

Terry Venables ‘I think it’s fifty-fifty.’

‘There’s nobody fitter at his age, except maybe Raquel Welch.’
– Ron Atkinson lauds Gordon Strachan, 39

‘Manchester United take on more in programme sales than we take on the gate.’
– Lawrie McMenemy, Southampton

‘If I walked on water, my accusers would say it is because I can’t swim.’
– Berti Vogts, Germany coach

‘You don’t have to have been a horse to be a jockey.’
– Arrigo Sacchi, Italy coach, defending a meagre playing record

‘Love is good for footballers, as long as it is not at half-time.’
– Richard Moller Nielsen, Denmark coach

‘I was about to say, before something far more interesting interrupted ...’
– John Motson, France vs Bulgaria

‘Why didn’t you just belt it, son?’
– Gareth Southgate’s mother reflects publicly on her son’s penalty miss

‘The only way we will be going to Europe is if the club splash out and take us all to Euro Disney.’
– Dean Holdsworth, Wimbledon

‘I was shocked when I was first introduced to the fans because they brought out a sheep, cut its head off and smeared blood all over my forehead.’
– Manchester United’s Ronnie Johnson on life with Besikts, Turkey

‘If the players want to make it hard for me, I am happy to make it twice as hard for them.’

– Wendy Tims, the first female referee to officiate in a professional game

‘The score is Sunderland nil, Leicester nil, the temperature is nil and the entertainment value is not much above nil.’

– Sunderland vs Leicester, Radio 5 Live

‘I think having Wasps around here as well gives us that little buzz around the place.’

– Ray Wilkins on the QPR–Wasps groundshare

‘This is an unusual Scotland side because they have good players.’

– Praise for the Under-21s from Javier Clemente, Spain’s coach

‘There are some great defenders here, I just don’t know their names.’

– David Ginola of Newcastle and France

‘It took a lot of bottle for Tony to own up.’

– Ian Wright on the Arsenal captain’s confession to alcoholism

‘It’s sods law. Now I’ve got time to improve my golf it’s the wrong time of year.’

– Howard Wilkinson when sacked by Leeds

‘I know where he should have put his flag up, and he’d have got plenty of help.’

– Ron Atkinson at Stamford Bridge

‘The referee was booking everyone. I thought he was filling in his lottery numbers.’

– Ian Wright

‘Asking Ruud Gullit to perform in this sort of match is like asking Kiri te Kanawa to jam with the Spice Girls.’

– Radio 5 Live’s Pat Murphy on the lousy pitch at Derby and the ill-tempered nature of the game

‘Pires has got something about him, he can go both ways depending on who’s facing him.’

– David Pleat

'Batistuta gets most of his goals with the ball.'
– Ian St John

'The good news for Nigeria is that they're 2–0 down very early in the game.'
– Kevin Keegan

'Moreano thought that the fullback was gonna come up behind and give him one really hard.'
– Big Ron

'Adams is stretching himself, looking for Seaman.'
– Brian Moore

'I wouldn't be surprised if this game went all the way to the finish.'
– Ian St John

'Apart from their goals, Norway haven't scored.'
– Terry Venables

'The Croatians don't play well without the ball.'
– Barry Venison

'It had to go in, but it didn't.'
– Peter Drury

'That's lifted the crowd up into the air.'
– Barry Davies

'He never fails to hit the target. But that was a miss.'
– Bobby Robson

'Batistuta is very good at pulling off defenders.'
– Kevin Keegan

Kevin Keegan 'Only one team can win this game ... and that team is England.'

Brian Moore 'But wait a minute, here's Dan Petrescu ...'

'Chile have three options – they could win or they could lose.'
– Kevin Keegan

‘That would have been a goal if the goalkeeper hadn’t saved it.’

– Kevin Keegan

‘I came to Nantes two years ago and it’s much the same today, except that it’s completely different.’

– Kevin Keegan

‘A tremendous strike which hit the defender full on the arm – and it nearly came off.’

– Kevin Keegan

‘Zidane is not very happy, because he is suffering from the wind.’

– Ron Atkinson

‘They’ve picked their heads up off the ground and they now have a lot to carry on their shoulders.’

– Ron Atkinson

‘He sliced the ball when he had it on a plate.’

– Ron Atkinson

‘I’m afraid they’ve left their legs at home.’

– Ron Atkinson

‘The new West Stand casts a giant shadow over the entire pitch, even on a sunny day.’

– Chris Jones, Evening Standard

‘Unfortunately, we keep kicking ourselves in the foot.’

– Ray Wilkins, BBC1

‘I’ve got a gut feeling in my stomach …’

– Alan Sugar, BBC1

‘Johnson has revelled in the “hole” behind Dwight Yorke …’

– Carling FA Premiership www page

‘An inch or two either side of the post and that would have been a goal.’

– Dave Bassett, Sky Sports

‘Both sides have scored a couple of goals and both sides have conceded a couple of goals.’

– Peter With, Radio 5 Live

'You don't score 64 goals in 86 games at the highest level without being able to score goals.'

– Alan Green, Radio 5 Live

'What's it like being in Bethlehem, the place where Christmas began? I suppose it's like seeing Ian Wright at Arsenal ...'

– Simon Fanshawe, Talk Radio

'And we all know that in football if you stand still you go backwards ...'

– Peter Reid, Tyne Tees Sport Special

'The lad got all over-excited when he saw the whites of the goalpost's eyes.'

– Steve Coppel, Radio 5 Live

'They (Rosenborg) have won 66 games, and they've scored in all of them.'

– Brian Moore, ITV

'The lads really ran their socks into the ground.'

– Alex Ferguson

'He (Brian Laudrup) wasn't just facing one defender – he was facing one at the front and one at the back as well.'

– Trevor Steven, STV

'... but Arsenal are quick to credit Bergkamp with laying on 75 percent of their nine goals.'

– Tony Gubba, BBC Match of the Day

'... an excellent player (Ian Wright) but he does have a black side.'

– Gary Lineker, BBC

'We say "educated left foot" ... Of course, there are many players with educated right foots.'

– Ron Jones, Radio 5 Live

'That's twice now he (Terry Phelan) has got between himself and the goal.'

– Brian Marwood, Radio 5 Live

'Mark Huges at his very best: he loves to feel people right behind him ...'

– Kevin Keegan

'We throw our dice into the ring and turned up trumps.'

– Bruce Rioch, ITV

'And I suppose they (Spurs) are nearer to being out of the FA Cup now than at any other time since the first half of this season, when they weren't ever in it anyway.'

– John Motson, BBC

'... and he crosses the line with the ball almost mesmerically tied to his foot with a ball of string ...'

– Ian Darke, Radio 5

'They've now got Ben Younes, Ben Ahmed and Ben Slimane. I think we'll have to stick to using just their surnames.'

– Motty on form in the Columbia vs Tunisia game, after Tunisia made a substitution

'He had to cut back inside onto his left foot because he literally hasn't got a right foot.'

– David Pleat during the United States' game against Iran

'It's men against boys. No, it's GODS against boys!'

– Clive Tyldesley gets over-excited during a Brazil vs Morocco game

'Brazil have only lost five times in their last 50 games; they lost 1–0 to the USA on a hot night in Athens, Georgia, home of the rock band REM (pause). Everybody hurts (pause) sometimes.'

– Clive Tyldesley during a Brazil vs Morocco game

Motty 'Well, I wonder what card the ref will show this time?'

Chris Waddle 'Well, with the going so far it could be a joker!'

Kevin Keegan does TV punditry proud again. Probably meaning to say something along the lines of 'too many chiefs, not enough Indians' he came out with: 'Sometimes there are too many generals and not enough, er, people waving to the generals as they, er, walk past.'

Justplain Darren & Friends Profile
Mark Fish

Favourite personal sporting memory?	I have been fortunate enough to have had many wonderful memories from the sporting fields over the years. The 1996 African Cup of Nations was probably one of the biggest highlights of my sporting life, as it was really that tournament that catapulted me into the limelight and onto some of the world's greatest footballing stages, which in turn provided me with many of the opportunities that I am fortunate to have in my life today
What's your idea of a perfect weekend?	A weekend at a nudist colony with my wife
What would be the best way for a fan to approach you in a bar?	With a couple of drinks in their hand – I never say no to a drink or two ...
What do you refuse to pay for?	I would like to refuse to pay for my wife's shopping, but she always seems to leave her purse at home when we go shopping
Tell us a secret of your trade?	If I told you, it wouldn't be a secret, would it ...?
Have you ever been arrested? And for what?	Yes. For being caught in possession of good looks. They told me that they would release me on bail if I could get someone ugly to bail me out, but unfortunately Darren wasn't available
What's been the lowest task/job you've ever had to perform?	I was once asked to make an appearance in an UNDERGROUND parking lot at a shopping centre – that was quite low
What will always be in your fridge?	A cold Castle and a bottle of champagne
Favourite 'junk food' meal?	Believe it or not, I generally do not eat junk food
What's the last drink you have before going to bed at night?	I usually cannot remember whether it is the eighth or ninth one ...

What's your biggest indulgence?	Scuba-diving
Best advice given to you by your mother?	'If you go out at night and you are not in bed by midnight, go home.'
What would your profession be if you were not a professional sportsman?	A wine farmer or professional wine taster
There are Seven Wonders of the World, what's your eighth?	My wife
Your Top 5 list of music?	U2 Red Hot Chili Peppers Lenny Kravitz REM Smashing Pumpkins
Best 'chirp' you have heard during a sports event?	As a young footballer I once heard an opposition defender say to my fellow striker that he was the ugliest punter he had ever seen, to which my fellow striker responded that that was not what the defender's missus had said the night before
Who is your mentor/hero?	Nelson Mandela is both my hero and mentor. He is one of few people who have truly earned my respect
If you could swap places with anyone for a day who would it be, and why?	My wife, so I can go out and spend my own money for a change
A quote or phrase that has had an impact on your life or best describes you?	You get out of life what you put into it
A one-liner that best describes Darren and his radio show?	Four hours of quality, fun-filled entertainment

Football Jokes

Q. Why do Brazilians make great lovers?
A. Because they can lob Seaman at 30 yards ...

Q. Why aren't the England football team allowed to own a dog?
A. Because they can't hold on to a lead.

Q. What's the difference between the England team and a tea bag?
A. The tea bag stays in the cup longer.

Q. What's the difference between a packet of Sellotape and Nicky Butt?
A. One's a glueless kit.

Q. What do you call an Englishman in the World Cup?
A. Ref.

Q. What is the main function of the England coach?
A. To transport the team from the hotel to the ground.

Q. What's the England version of a hat-trick?
A. Conceding three goals in fifteen minutes.

Q. What's the most proficient form of footwork displayed by the England midfielders?
A. The walk back to the dressing room.

Q. What do Heskey and drug addicts have in common?
A. Both spend most of their time wondering where their next score will come from.

Q. How does Beckham change a light bulb?
A. He holds it in the air, and the world revolves around him.

Oxo were going to bring out a World Cup commemorative cube painted red, white and blue in honour of the England squad.

But it was a laughing stock and crumbled in the box.

Rumours that David Beckham was seen successfully seducing a young woman in a nightclub with a one-liner have been completely refuted by the English FA. England's chief publicity officer stated: 'I find it totally preposterous to suggest that one of our players could make a successful pass to or at anyone.'

Beckham, Keane and Ferguson are all trapped on the roof of a burning building. The Fire Brigade duly arrive and hold out the big blanket for the guys to jump onto.

The are understandably all a bit nervous but, being a brave lad and the club captain, Keane goes first. At the last second, the firemen whip the blanket away. Keane splats on the pavement, dead. Still giggling, the firemen shout to Ferguson to go next. He jumps, they move the blanket, and he makes a pancake on the pavement. High fives all around from the firemen. Last to go is Beckham. But he's not having any of it ...

'You'll move the blanket!' he shouts.

'No we won't,' they reply.

'It's no good, I don't trust you. You'll move the blanket again!' shouts Becks. 'Come on, jump you fool!' they shout.

'Well, alright,' he replies. 'But I'm not jumping until you put the blanket down and move away from it ...'

Fabien Barthez is ill, so Alex Ferguson offers to go shopping for him. While in the local supermarket, he bumps into Gerard Houllier.

'Hello, Alex, what are you doing here?'

'I'm getting a bag of potatoes for Fabien Barthez.'

'Sounds like a fair swap to me!!'

David Beckham is visiting a school. In one class, he asks the students if anyone can give him an example of a 'tragedy'. One little boy stands up and offers that if my best friend who lives next door was playing in the street and a car came along and killed him, that would be a tragedy.

'No,' Beckham says, 'that would be an ACCIDENT.'

A girl raises her hand.

'If a school bus carrying fifty children drove off a cliff, killing everyone involved ... that would be a tragedy.'

'I'm afraid not,' explains Beckham. 'That is what we would call a GREAT LOSS.'

The room is silent; none of the children volunteer.

'What?' asks Beckham. 'Isn't there anyone here who can give me an example of a tragedy?'

Finally a boy in the back raises his hand. In a timid voice he says, 'If an airplane carrying David Beckham was blown up by a bomb, *that* would be a tragedy.'

Beckham beams. 'Marvellous! And can you tell me WHY that would be a tragedy?'

'Well,' says the boy, 'because it wouldn't be an accident and it certainly wouldn't be a great loss.'

Two boys are playing football in a park in London. Suddenly a dog appears and sinks its teeth into the younger boy's chest. The elder picks up a stick and drives it through the dog's ear, killing it.

A reporter observes all of this and asks the boy if he can write a story on it. He takes out a notebook and puts down the title:

'ARSENAL FAN SAVES FRIEND'S LIFE'

The boy says, 'I don't support Arsenal,' so the reporter puts down:

'CHELSEA FAN SAVES FRIEND'S LIFE'

The boy says, 'I don't support Chelsea.'

So the reporter asks, 'Who do you support?'

'Manchester United,' replies the boy.

So the reporter writes down:

'GLORY-HUNTING IDIOT KILLS FAMILY PET'

Chelsea and Manchester United are playing at Stamford Bridge. George Weah, the Chelsea striker, is fouled by Jaap Stam. He stands up and protests loudly to the ref. David Beckham runs up to Weah, puts his finger to his lips and says: *sssshhhh*!

After 20 minutes a defensive blunder by the Chelsea back four lets in Andy Cole to put Manchester United 1–0 up. George Weah screams at the defenders and tells them to wake up. Beckham again approaches Weah, puts his finger to his lips and says: *ssshhh*! Then he bursts out laughing and returns to his position.

Just before half-time Weah is caught offside by the linesman. Again he is very loud and vocal in his protest. Once again Beckham runs over to Weah and repeats his gesture … *sssshhhh*! Everyone is confused by his actions, and at half-time Roy Keane goes over to Becks and enquires about the fingers to the lips, etc. Beckham whispers something to Keane who stands back, rolls his eyes and says to Beckham, 'You idiot, Beckham – he's a *Liberian*!

Cindy Crawford, Bill Gates and Osama Bin Laden are hanging out.

Cindy says, 'I'm the most beautiful girl in the world.'

Bill Gates says, 'I'm the richest man in the world.'

Osama bin Laden says, 'I'm the most hated man in the world.'

They are all very proud of their assertions.

Cindy Crawford says, 'I've got a truth mirror in my house. It gives you all the truthful answers. Wanna see it?'

So they all go to Cindy's house.

Cindy comes out two minutes later. She is happy, and she says, 'I am right! The mirror of truth says I'm the most beautiful girl in the world!'

Five minutes later, Bill Gates comes out. He is happy, and he says, 'I'm right! The mirror of truth says I'm the richest dude in the world!'

Ten minutes later, Osama comes out. He is furious. He says, 'WHO THE HELL IS ALEX FERGUSON !???!!!'

Albert Einstein arrives at a party and introduces himself to the first person he sees, and asks, 'What is your IQ?' The man answers, '241.'

'That is wonderful!' says Albert. 'We will talk about the Grand Unification Theory and the mysteries of the Universe. We will have much to discuss!'

Next Albert introduces himself to a woman and asks, 'What is your IQ?'

The lady answers, '144.'

'That is great!' responds Albert. 'We can discuss politics and current affairs. We will have much to discuss!'

Albert then goes to another person and asks, 'What is your IQ?'

The man answers, '6.'

Albert says, 'How is Manchester United doing this season?'

Posh Spice was driving home and got caught in a really bad hailstorm.

Her car was covered with dents, so the next day she took it to the local garage. The garage owner saw who she was and decided to have some fun.

He told her to go home and blow into the exhaust pipe really hard, and all the dents would pop out.

So, the thin-as-you-like popstrel went home, got down on her hands and knees and started blowing into the tailpipe. Nothing happened. She blew a little harder and still nothing happened.

Floppy haired hacker Beckham, upon hearing the huffing and puffing from outside the house, pulled a tracksuit over the skimpy knickers and peephole bra he was wearing and went into the courtyard.

'What are you doing?' asked Becks.

Posh then told him how the repairman had instructed her to blow in the exhaust in order to get all the dents to pop out.

Beckham, clearly shocked at Posh's stupidity, rolled his eyes.

'Duh! You need to roll up the windows first!'

Posh Spice decided to help benefit the community and began a job as a primary school counsellor. One day during break time she noticed a boy standing by himself on the side of the playing field while the rest of the kids enjoyed a game of football at the other end.

Knowing a little bit about football through her marriage, she decided to have a conversation with him. So she approached and asked if he was all right, in the knowledge that if he wasn't she could talk to him about the game.

The boy said he was OK. A little while later, however, she noticed the boy was in the same spot, still by himself, watching the game.

Approaching again, Victoria said, 'Would you like me to be your friend?'

The boy hesitated, then said, 'OK,' looking at the woman suspiciously.

Feeling she was making progress, she then asked, 'Why are you standing here alone?'

'Because,' the little boy said with great exasperation, 'I'm the f^^^ing goalkeeper – now piss off.'

An antique collector walks into a store in a place called Hamlyn. He sees a small brass rat on the shelf. After looking for any other bargains in the store, he decides he wants to buy the rat. He asks the storekeeper, 'How much for the brass rat?'

The storekeeper says, 'Ten marks for the rat. One hundred and twenty marks for the story.'

The guy asks, 'What's the story?'

The storekeeper says, 'I won't tell you unless you give me a hundred and twenty marks.'

The collector says, 'Skip the story,' pays for the rat, and walks out of the store. He puts the rat in his backpack and starts riding his bike across the nearest bridge. A short time later the guy looks behind him, and sees a rat following him. This strikes him as odd, but not unheard of, so he pedals on. A moment later he hears cars honking behind him, and turns around to see a pack of about a dozen rats following him. He turns and pedals faster. Finally, as he nears the other side of the bridge, he looks behind him and sees hundreds of rats chasing him. He concludes that the rats must be chasing the brass rat and decides this is too much. He stops his bike, pulls the rat from his pack and throws it off the bridge into the river. He watches as the huge pack of rats jump off the bridge and drown. Relieved but curious, the guy pedals back to the antique store. The storekeeper sees him come in, shakes his head, and says, 'You should have bought the story. You can still have it for one hundred and twenty marks.'

The guy shakes his head and says, 'Forget the story. How much for the brass Manchester United supporter?'

YOU DON'T HAVE TO BE POSH TO SWALLOW BECKS
– Becks Beer advert

Darren's Travel Arrangements

My birthday is on the 26th of January … Every year! I know this is on my profile and probably elsewhere in this book, but it's always good to let people know when you celebrate a birthday … that's 26 January, then.

This year's birthday had to be the strangest I've ever had. Normally I'd be at home or maybe in some exotic South African place like Durban or Bloem, but this year it happened to coincide with our 5fm team-building weekend. So, I spent my birthday in a Bedouin tent amongst the sand dunes of Swakopmund, Namibia!

What a strange place as well! Looks like some German town that was picked up by a tornado and dumped in the Namib desert. How I got there, though, is another, typical, Justplain story …

For the team-building weekend, the station management wanted us all to travel as a team, all on the same flight. The flight was to leave on the Friday morning at 10.40, Jo'burg to Walvis Bay, and bus from WB to Swakop. Of course, that meant being at the airport no later than an hour before departure, i.e. 9.40 am. Of this point I was reminded in no uncertain terms, on numerous occasions, and by each and every member of our 5fm travelling party! (Obviously, they had some or other misguided impression that I am a habitual flight-misser and serial oversleeper/latecomer … pah!). Or maybe they were aware of the fact that I had a massive *Cosmo* function the night before and know that I tend to thrive at massive functions and sometimes don't get home before sunrise.

I didn't.

Having arrived home at about 6.30 am (great party) I decided not to go to sleep, but instead just to stay awake and amuse myself until about 8.00 am, at which time I would leave for the airport and stun all my colleagues by being the first to check in. It was while contemplating this idea that I fell asleep.

There was only the one flight to Walvis that day. This I found out after answering my home phone (cellphone battery dead) at about 9.45 am. It was the boss! Everyone had checked in, and I had overslept! I was a &@$&>%$ and &@$&>%$, and not to mention a &@$&>%$. I kind of assumed that following that conversation, I probably wasn't very welcome on the team-building trip any more, anyway. The rest of the guys assumed that I wasn't coming any more, now that I wasn't going to make my flight, and prepared themselves for a Scott-free weekend (which roughly translates to a weekend of less suitcases, Jack Daniels, vulgar and sexist comments and practical jokes). How wrong they were!

I asked my assistant to find some way of getting me to Swakop that day, and she did. I could fly to Windhoek at noon, but would have to catch a charter from Windhoek straight into Swakop. There were two things wrong with this scenario: firstly, I hate flying (oh, yes), and the prospect of a single-engine aeroplane taking me across a desert wasn't an enticing one. Secondly, a charter would set me back about R5 000!

I had no choice, and decided to take that option. Then I worked out that if one compared my route to my colleagues', there was a good chance that I could actually arrive at the hotel before the rest of them! This had now become a challenge … I wanted to see the faces of the guys who thought I wasn't coming at all when they arrived at the hotel to see me sitting in reception, sipping a Jack on the rocks and puffing on a Marlboro.

After an uneventful flight to Windhoek I was actually ahead of schedule … now I had to find the pilot of my charter. Because we had landed 30 minutes ahead of schedule in Windhoek, I had to wait for half an hour before he arrived, which, as it turned out, put paid to my plan to surprise my mates. When he did arrive, I almost fell over! He didn't look a day over 12 years old! As we walked to the plane, I nervously asked him all the questions that nervous flyers ask their pilots: is the weather on route OK? What percentage of successful landings have you completed? What percentage of successful landings has your plane completed? Do you drink? How the hell old ARE you really??? And he answered them with a pilot's usual aplomb … There are thunderstorms in the area; the plane has had a few technical problems, but we'll give it a bash anyway; maybe you should take a sick pill and get very drunk cos this one is gonna be f*****g bumpy! etc., etc.

As it turns out, he wasn't the pilot … just co-pilot. No, the pilot looked much older … about 16! When I had landed I spotted what I thought looked like my R5 000 charter standing on the runway … Twin engine, 10-seater … looked OK. As it turns out, R5 000 doesn't get you much by way of planes these days! As I got into the four-seater single-engine vomit-comet, I smashed two VERY stiff (double) tots of Jack, and wedged myself into my seat … and prayed.

The flight was actually an absolute jol. We circumnavigated the storms, I had another five or six Jacks and got into a VERY good mood. My pilots were *Boots and All* addicts (which is a good thing cos no pilot wants to have the mantle of being the guy who killed a *Boots and All* presenter …) and we landed safely in Swakop an hour or so later.

Had it not been for the half hour wasted waiting for the pilots to arrive in Windhoek, and the other half hour I spent waiting at Swakopmund Airport for the hotel transport to fetch me, I would easily have beaten my colleagues to the hotel. Fact is, I arrived at reception literally seconds after their bus had pulled off to take them into the dunes for the first team-building activities.

On the way to meet up with them, my phone rang. It was Jonty Rhodes over in Adelaide, Aus-*spit*-stralia, wanting to know why I wasn't on air (we had stand-ins working whilst we were on team-building), cos he had just figured out how to hook up to 5fm's streaming audio (bandwidth by Megawan), and was listening on his computer in his Adelaide hotel room! At that moment I marvelled at how far technology had come … There I was sitting in the middle of a desert in Namibia, talking to a guy in Adelaide who could hear that I wasn't on the air from the studio in Johannesburg!!

Despite the fact that I didn't beat the gang to the site, the 'How the hell …?' and 'What the …?' expressions on their faces were priceless when they saw me wandering towards them in the desert like the prodigal son coming home …

Many suitcases and Jacks were polished off in between those dunes that weekend, I tell you …

Justplain's average air ticket

Note the time Darren initially intended travelling from Cape Town to Johannesburg. Thereafter his flight times were changed at regular intervals until he took flight SA 347. Considering that he left Cape Town at 2 pm and it takes two hours to Johannesburg, one can only wonder what time he was 'actually' on air, as the Justplain Show starts at 3 pm.

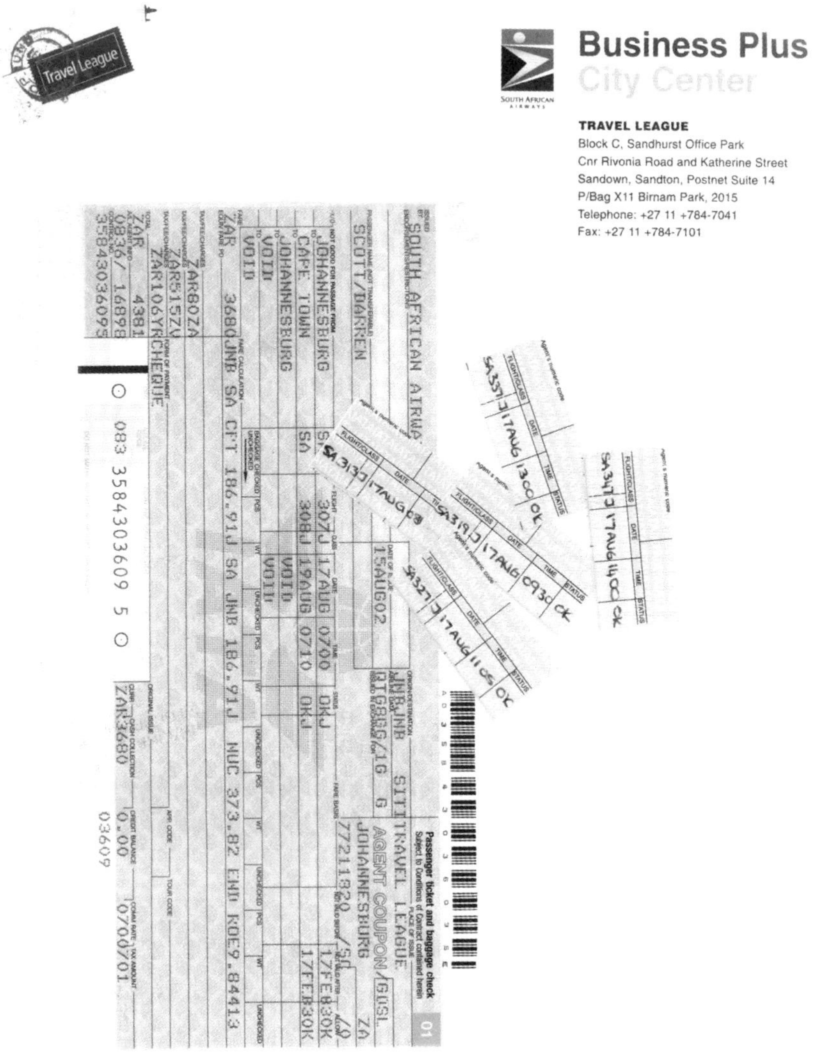

The Justplain Excuse List

These are reasons given to Ian F why Darren was late for his radio show:

- The traffic was backed up all the way to my house.
- There was lots of air traffic over Johannesburg.
- The pilot didn't take the shortest route to Johannesburg; that's why the flight was delayed.
- Just come out of meeting and was parked in. On my way.
- Caught a late flight. I'll be fifteen minutes late.
- On my way from airport coming back from Durban. Late again Bob!
- Caught a late flight … to Cape Town … Will be an hour late … oops!
- Late from golf. Had a shower …
- No one told me about my radio show today!! It's not in my diary.
- I've been in an edit all night – didn't know it was so late already.
- It's not three o'clock *already*, is it?

Justplain Darren & Friends Profile
Ian F

Favourite personal sporting memory?	For me, getting onto 5fm has to be the highlight of my career. It was the start as well … and I got a chance to work with Plain … Nice!
What's your idea of a perfect weekend?	Spending time in the bush has to be my perfect weekend away. I love the bush!
What would be the best way for a fan to approach you in a bar?	I am not impressed by job status. I love people, and if anyone approaches me, I love to chat … simple as that!
What do you refuse to pay for?	Bad service
Tell us a secret of your trade?	
Have you ever been arrested? And for what?	No … never!
What's been the lowest task/job you've ever had to perform?	Compost loader at a nursery!
What will always be in your fridge?	Chillies
Favourite 'junk food' meal?	Nandos
What's the last drink you have before going to bed at night?	If it's been a heavy night … Jack Daniels. A good chilled night, Thelema Cabernet Sauvignon
What's your biggest indulgence?	Music

Best advice given to you by your mother?	Remember the consequences
What would your profession be if you were not a professional radio DJ?	A pilot!
There are Seven Wonders of the World, what's your eighth?	MIDI
Your Top 5 list of music?	William Orbit – Water From a Vine Leaf The Orb – Little Fluffy Clouds Chicane – Don't Give Up Sunscreem – Love You More Oystein Sevag – There's a Monk in My Garden
Best 'chirp' you have heard during a sports event?	
Who is your mentor/hero?	Alex Jay
If you could swap places with anyone for a day who would it be, and why?	Michael Schumacher … DUH!!!!
A quote or phrase that has had an impact on your life or best describes you?	
A one-liner that best describes Darren and his radio show?	Late again!!!!

Justplain Darren & Friends Profile
Sasha Martinengo

Favourite personal sporting memory?	Well, from school it must have been when I was made captain of rugby, cricket and house captain for my Matric year. I think having had those responsibilities led to me being able to deal with people later in life. Other than that, I love all sports and get emotional at just about every occasion. Most notably must be South Africa winning the Rugby World Cup, Italy winning the Soccer World Cup in 1982 and then of course Michael Schumacher winning the driver's title in 2000
What's your idea of a perfect weekend?	Lots of great sex and sport or sport then sex; either way as long as they are both good, then I am happy **To put in order:** Sex Rugby match Sex Rugby match Lunch Sex F1 Grand Prix Jubilant Sex One-Day Cricket Match Sex Golf tournament No more sex because I am the only one awake by that time
What would be the best way for a fan to approach you in a bar?	Don't. No, seriously, I think people should just respect 'personalities' and if they want to have a word with them, then be diplomatic and tactful
What do you refuse to pay for?	I am usually the sucker that pays for everything, especially for those who refuse to pay for something
Tell us a secret of your trade?	No secrets, just continuous hard work and research
Have you ever been arrested? And for what?	Yes. Not paying traffic offences. They arrested me at my house at 7 am and dragged me off to the courts. It was surreal; there I was in a court jail with convicted murderers, etc. and I was in for not paying some speeding fines. My mother had to come and bail me out
What's been the lowest task/job you've ever had to perform?	Easy. Cleaning bathrooms during my military stint. But also, I had to make coffee for Darren once

What will always be in your fridge? Favourite 'junk food' meal?	Milk, Coca-Cola and Ice Pizza, although that is not junk food to me. Also, schwarmas
What's the last drink you have before going to bed at night?	Usually a cold drink but if it's been a heavy night then a litre of water
What's your biggest indulgence?	Formula 1 merchandise. Spending money on my Slot Car Race Track and the biggest is spending money on my wife and kids
Best advice given to you by your mother?	If you're not in bed by 10, go home
What would your profession be if you were not a professional correspondent?	Car wash owner with an Espresso coffee shop all in one. Anyone wanna invest?
There are Seven Wonders of the World, what's your eighth?	What are the seven? Let me think … perhaps the truth behind all of the seven. I would love to know the TRUTH
Your Top 5 list of music?	Journey – Faithfully Robert Miles – Children William Orbit – Water from a Vine Leaf Pavarotti – Caruso Michael Jackson – Will You Be There
Best 'chirp' you have heard during a sports event?	'Rubens, move over' – hahahaha. OK, wow, there are many and I can't think of any
Who is your mentor/hero?	My father
If you could swap places with anyone for a day who would it be, and why?	God, to know it all
A quote or phrase that has had an impact on your life or best describes you?	Keep The Passion! (Best describes me) Avoid having your ego so close to your position that when your position falls, your ego goes with it. And basically everything my father and mother still teach me about life has helped me in my development
A one-liner that best describes Darren and his radio show?	This is going to be a long line. I have been very fortunate to work with Darren on 5fm, to me he is an inspiration; he has his moods but he is one of the most creative people I have ever met and to me his show is the best on any radio station. I am not saying that for the sake of this article, but purely because I mean it. He has more talent than most DJs put together. He is one of the most generous individuals I have ever met and I am privileged to know and work with him

Formula 1 Trivia

1. What was the first Formula 1 Grand Prix that Michael Schumacher won?
2. Ferrari won the constructors' world championship in 2000 after quite a lengthy dry spell. How many years had it been?
3. Who are the principal lubricant and fuel sponsors of the Ferrari team for 2001?
4. How many races did the McLaren team win in 1988?
5. Who won the Formula 1 drivers' championship in 1950?
6. Who holds the record for the most pole positions?
7. Who was the youngest ever Formula 1 champion?
8. Who won the Formula 1 drivers' championship in 1979?
9. In what year did Ayrton Senna die?
10. What does Heinz-Harald Frentzen's father do for a living?
11. Who are the current drivers for the Ferrari team?
12. How many GPs has David Coulthard won in his career so far?
13. Which constructor won the championship from 1988 to 1991?
14. In what year did Juan-Manuel Fangio win his first championship?
15. How many GPs did Alain Prost win?
16. Murray Walker first commentated on the British Grand Prix in which year?
17. At which circuit did Gilles Villeneuve lose his life?
18. What make of car did Jochen Rindt win the world championship in?

19. How many points did Jacques Villeneuve score in the 2000 season?
20. What nationality is Phil Hill, the 1961 world champion?
21. During the qualifying round on Saturday, how many laps is each driver allowed, and which one counts towards his ultimate grid position for Sunday's race?
22. How many GPs did the Toleman team compete in?
23. How many GPs have taken place in South Africa?
24. Which current Formula 1 driver won the 1993 Le Mans 24-hour race in the GT class?
25. Who won the drivers' championship in 1999?
26. Who is the head of the FIA?
27. What is the name of the South African chief designer of the Ferrari team?
28. In 1959 Jack Brabham won the Formula 1 championship in the Cooper T51. What was special about his championship win?
29. Who won the 2000 Australian Grand Prix?
30. Which teams did not score points during 2000?
31. Who won the inaugural Malaysian Grand Prix in 1999?
32. Jean Alesi has won one Grand Prix. Where was it and in what year?
33. How many points was a win worth in 1985?
34. Which team built the first carbon-fibre car in 1981?
35. Which works engine manufacturer marks their return to Formula 1 in 2001?
36. Who replaced Gilles Villeneuve at Ferrari after his death in 1982?

37. What make of car did Guiseppe Farina drive in 1950?

38. Which driver holds the record for the most world championship titles – five in all?

39. For which team did Jacques Villeneuve start his Formula 1 career?

40. Alex Yoong is the first Formula 1 driver from which country?

41. If the track-side marshals are waving a blue flag, what does it mean?

42. How many times has the Williams team won the constructors' championship?

43. Which driver holds the record for taking part in the most Grand Prix – 256 of them?

44. In what year did the constructors' championship start?

45. Who has been the youngest winner of a GP?

46. What make of fuel does the Ferrari team use?

47. When was Ayrton Senna's last win?

48. Who replaced Michael Schumacher in 1999 when he broke his legs?

49. Who was known as 'the Professor'?

50. Who won the Formula 1 drivers' championship in 1996?

51. If the track-side marshals are waving a black flag with an orange spot and a number on it, what does it mean?

52. Who holds the record for qualifying in pole position 14 times in one season?

53. Who were the drivers for the Jordan team in 2001?

54. What are the names of the two tyre manufacturers in Formula 1?

55. Of all the current drivers in Formula 1, who is the oldest?

56. Which race did McLaren not win in 1988?

57. What engine did the Ferrari team use in 1957?

58. Who won the drivers' championship in 1971?

59. Which driver was only issued with a 'temporary' Formula 1 license before his debut season, as he was considered too inexperienced?

60. Which team has Eddie Irvine not driven for?

61. Olivier Panis' only Grand Prix win came in 1996. Which one was it?

62. Which driver holds the world record for having driven for the most Formula 1 teams in his career – 13 in all, from 1963 to 1976?

63. Which team entered Formula 1 in 2002?

64. What is the name of the Finn who started driving for the Sauber team in 2001?

65. Which famous commentator retired recently?

Answers to FORMULA 1 TRIVIA on page 114

Justplain Darren & Friends Profile
Neil Mallard

Favourite personal sporting memory?	The 1970 Brazil vs Italy World Cup final. The greatest and best sports event I attended
What's your idea of a perfect weekend?	Sailing with the family off Cowes, Isle of Wight
What would be the best way for a fan to approach you in a bar?	Offer me a drink!
What do you refuse to pay for?	Sex
Tell us a secret of your trade?	Personal satisfaction
Have you ever been arrested? And for what?	Many times – usually in countries with the word 'Democratic' in their title
What's been the lowest task/job you've ever had to perform?	No job is too low if circumstances demand – unemployment is much worse
What will always be in your fridge?	Cheese
Favourite 'junk food' meal?	Four fried eggs and chips
What's the last drink you have before going to bed at night?	Wine – usually red
What's your biggest indulgence?	My yacht (and champagne)

Best advice given to you by your mother?	Watch out for your father!
What would your profession be if you were not a professional correspondent?	Sea Captain
There are Seven Wonders of the World, what's your eighth?	My South African wife of thirty-seven years
Your Top 5 list of music?	1. Tchaikovsky 2. Oscar Peterson 3. Mozart 4. The Modcan Jazz Quartet 5. The Travelling Wilburys
Best 'chirp' you have heard during a sports event?	What's a 'chirp'?
Who is your mentor/hero?	My first newspaper editor
If you could swap places with anyone for a day who would it be, and why?	Bernard Eccelstone. I would love to run the Grand Prix for one day – but no longer!
A quote or phrase that has had an impact on your life or best describes you?	A well-prepared professional always succeeds
A one-liner that best describes Darren and his radio show?	Comprehensive, Riveting And Professional

Formula 1 Quotes

'Never think of your car as a cold machine, but as a hot-blooded horse.'
– Juan-Manuel Fangio, 1958

'It is like balancing an egg on a spoon while shooting rapids.'
– Graham Hill describing Formula One racing

'Even in moments of tranquillity, Murray Walker sounds like a man whose trousers are on fire.'
– Clive James, Australian broadcaster

'Well, he's world champion, and we only get one of those a year.'
– Murray Walker

'Only a few more laps to go and then the action will begin, unless this is the action, which it is.'
– Murray Walker

'I should imagine that the conditions in the cockpit are unimaginable!'
– Murray Walker

'Nigel Mansell – the man of the race – the man of the day – the man from the Isle of Man.'
– Murray Walker

'The lead car is absolutely unique except for the one behind it.'
– Murray Walker

'We now have exactly the same situation as we had at the start of the race, only exactly the opposite.'
– Murray Walker

'Just under 10 seconds for Nigel Mansell. Call it 9.5 seconds in round numbers.'
– Murray Walker

'Do my eyes deceive me, or is Senna's car sounding a bit rough?'
– Murray Walker

Golf Quotes

'The only way of really finding out a man's true character is to play golf with him.'

– **PG Wodehouse**

'Golf is a game whose aim is to hit a very small ball into an even smaller hole with weapons singularly ill-designed for that purpose.'

– **Winston Churchill**

'Golf is 20 percent mechanics and technique. The other 80 percent is philosophy, humour, tragedy, romance, melodrama, companionship, camaraderie, cussedness and conversation.'

– **Grantland Rice**

'We speak of eyeball-to-eyeball encounters between men great and small. Even more reaching and revealing of character is the eyeball-to-golfball confrontation, whereby our most secret natures are mercilessly tested by a small, round, whitish object with no mind or will but with a very definite life of its own, and with whims perverse and beatific.'

– **John Stewart Martin**

'Golf puts a man's character on the anvil and his richest qualities – patience, poise and restraint – to the flame.'

– **Billy Casper**

'Nothing dissects a man in public quite like golf.'

– **Brent Musberger**

'I play golf with friends, but we do not play friendly games.'

– **Ben Hogan**

'It is almost impossible to remember how tragic a place the world is when one is playing golf.'

– **Robert Lynd**

'A good foundation is the first thing that is built when a house is constructed. In the same way, one needs to get a good foundation before you swing the club – this starts with a good grip, good alignment and good stance and posture.'

– **Mark Immelman**

'One of the most fascinating things about golf is how it reflects the cycle of life. No matter what you shoot – the next day you have to go back to the first tee and begin all over again and make yourself into something.'

– Peter Jacobson

'If you drink, don't drive. Don't even putt.'

– Dean Martin, US film actor

'Seve's got shots the rest of us don't even know.'

– Ben Crenshaw referring to Seve Ballesteros

'These greens are so fast they must bikini wax them.'

– Gary McCord on the greens at Augusta

'One of the reasons Arnie [Arnold Palmer] is playing so well is that before each tee shot his wife takes out his balls and kisses them ... Oh, my God, what have I just said?'

– USTV commentator Jonny Huntridge

Answers to FORMULA 1 TRIVIA on page 106

1. Spa in Belgium 1992; **2.** Sixteen; **3.** Shell; **4.** Fifteen; **5.** Guiseppe Farina; **6.** Ayrton Senna; **7.** Emerson Fittipaldi; **8.** Jody Scheckter; **9.** 1994; **10.** He's an undertaker; **11.** Rubens Barrichello and Michael Schumacher; **12.** Nine; **13.** McLaren; **14.** 1951; **15.** 51; **16.** 1949; **17.** Zolder; **18.** Lotus; **19.** Seventeen; **20.** American; **21.** Twelve, the fastest; **22.** 57; **23.** 23; **24.** David Coulthard; **25.** Mika Hakkinen; **26.** Max Moseley; **27.** Rory Byrne; **28.** It was the first championship to be won in a rear-engined car; **29.** Michael Schumacher; **30.** Prost and Minardi; **31.** Eddie Irvine; **32.** Canada, 1995; **33.** Nine; **34.** McLaren; **35.** Renault; **36.** Patrick Tambay; **37.** Alfa Romeo; **38.** Juan-Manuel Fangio; **39.** Williams; **40.** Malaysia; **41.** Driver must allow a rival to overtake him; **42.** Nine; **43.** Ricardo Patrese; **44.** 1958; **45.** Bruce McLaren in 1959; **46.** Shell; **47.** Adelaide, 1993; **48.** Mika Salo; **49.** Alain Prost; **50.** Damon Hill; **51.** The driver indicated he has a dangerous fault that is affecting his car, and he must drive into the pits immediately; **52.** Nigel Mansell; **53.** Heinz-Harald Frentzen and Jarno Trulli; **54.** Michelin and Bridgestone; **55.** Eddie Irvine; **56.** Monza; **57.** Lancia DS50 V8; **58.** Jackie Stewart; **59.** Kimi Raikkonen; **60.** Williams; **61.** The Monaco Grand Prix; **62.** Chris Amon; **63.** Toyota; **64.** Kimi Raikkonen; **65.** Murray Walker

Golf Humour

Golfer: I've played so poorly all day; I think I'm going to go drown myself in that lake.
Caddy: I don't think you could keep your head down that long.

Golfer: I'd move heaven and earth to be able to break 100 on this course.
Caddy: Try heaven. You've already moved most of the earth.

Golfer: Well, Caddy, How do you like my game?
Caddy: Very good, Sir. But personally I prefer golf.

Golfer: Well, I have never played this badly before.
Caddy: I didn't realise you had played before, Sir?

Golfer: Caddy, do you think my game is improving?
Caddy: Oh, yes, Sir. You're missing the ball by much less than you used to!

Golfer: Please stop checking your watch all the time, Caddy. It's very distracting.
Caddy: This isn't a watch, Sir, it's a compass.

Golfer: Caddy, do you think it is a sin to play golf on Sunday?
Caddy: The way you play, Sir, it's a crime to play any day of the week!

Golfer: This golf is a funny game.
Caddy: It's not supposed to be.

Golfer: That can't be my ball, Caddy, it looks far too old.
Caddy: It's a long time since we started, Sir.

Golfer: This is the worst golf course I've ever played on!
Caddy: This isn't the golf course, Sir! We left that an hour ago.

Golfer: So you think I can get there with a 5-iron?
Caddy: Eventually.

Golfer: You've got to be the worst caddy in the world!
Caddy: I doubt it. That would be too much of a coincidence.

Justplain Darren & Friends Profile
Mark Immelman

Favourite personal sporting memory?	**General:** South Africa winning the Rugby World Cup in '95 **Personal:** Trevor Immelman, my brother, playing in his first US Masters tournament
What's your idea of a perfect weekend?	**Friday night:** Going out to a cool place for drinks and dinner with friends **Saturday:** Spending relaxing time in quiet surroundings with Tracy **Sunday:** Watching one of my professional clients shoot 66 to win the US Masters
What would be the best way for a fan to approach you in a bar?	Do not call me Trevor … and if you do call me Mark, do not open with some stupid chirp about golf or one of my golf clients. Buying me a drink is always a good one though
What do you refuse to pay for?	Golf equipment
Tell us a secret of your trade?	We golf instructors are bound to a code of secrecy … Just kidding, no secrets really. We have to be pretty transparent as honest communication is our business
Have you ever been arrested? And for what?	Seeing as I am currently based in the USA, I can plead the Fifth Amendment on that one. (Let's just say that college was a somewhat wild time …)
What's been the lowest task/job you've ever had to perform?	Packing and sorting boxes of clothes in a warehouse in London
What will always be in your fridge?	Milk, cheese and fruit
Favourite 'junk food' meal?	Hot Chilli Dogs
What's the last drink you have before going to bed at night?	Depends what night of the week it is: weekdays would be water, weekends could be anything, depends on my mood

What's your biggest indulgence?	Travelling to foreign destinations on a whim. Running a close second is the Isuzu Rodeo I am about to buy
Best advice given to you by your mother?	'Get over it and move on!'
What would your profession be if you were not a professional correspondent?	I would love to be a television personality or a movie star
There are Seven Wonders of the World, what's your eighth?	It's a toss-up: The Statue of Liberty in New York, or Big Ben and the Houses of Parliament on the Thames
Your Top 5 list of music?	(1.) Higher – Creed (2.) Even Flow – Pearl Jam (3.) Too Bad – Nickelback (4.) Drops of Jupiter – Train (5.) My Way (or the Highway) – Limp Bizkit
Best 'chirp' you have heard during a sports event?	To Mark O'Meara, from an inebriated gallery member on the Nedbank Million Dollar driving range: 'Hey, Mark, head up and force!'
Who is your mentor/hero?	I would count my collegiate golf coach, Earl Bagley, as a mentor, and my hero is Michael Jordan
If you could swap places with anyone for a day who would it be, and why?	George W Bush. To get a perspective of real pressure, that of being the leader of the Western world
A quote or phrase that has had an impact on your life or best describes you?	'I can do all things through Him that is my strength.'
A one-liner that best describes Darren and his radio show?	Entertaining, amusing and cutting edge – a leader in his field ... he is 'Justplain' Darren, one of a kind!

Golf Trivia

1. Which player played the most times in the World Match Play finals?
2. How many times did Bobby Locke win the British Open title?
3. How many times has Gary Player won the US Open?
4. In which year did the three greats win all four Majors?
5. Where did Gary Player win on the US PGA tour for the first time?
6. In which year did Ernie Els turn professional?
7. Who won the first Sunshine Tour tournament?
8. Who was the first player to win the Million Dollar Championship three times?
9. How many Majors has Gary Player won?
10. Who was the first South African to win the Million Dollar Championship?
11. Which players represented South Africa at the 1998/99 Alfred Dunhill Cup at St Andrews?
12. In which year did Ernie Els win the Junior World title in San Diego?
13. Who has won the most British Open titles?
14. Who was the first player to win the British Open three consecutive times?
15. Who is the only player to score two holes in one in a British Open tournament?
16. What trophy is given to the winner of the Masters?
17. Which Major could Arnold Palmer never win?
18. How many Grand Slam titles did Greg Norman win?
19. Who was the first South African to win the US Open?

20. How many strokes behind was Gary Player when he went into the final round of the 1978 Masters?
21. Which teams play the Ryder Cup?
22. What format is the Ryder Cup played over?
23. Who captained the 1999 Europe Ryder Cup team?
24. Who captained the 1999 American Ryder Cup team?
25. Which player scored the first hole in one in the Ryder Cup?
26. In which year was the Ryder Cup played in Scotland for the first time?
27. Which golfer is known as 'El Niño'?
28. If two players share a golf bag, what is the maximum number of clubs allowed in that bag?
29. Who is acknowledged as the 'Father of Golf' in the United States?
30. Who was the metal wood pioneer?
31. Which golf club has its own handicap system?
32. Who is the only player to lose two playoffs at the Masters?
33. How many pimples are there on a golf ball?
34. How many strokes did Herman Tissies take at the Postage Stamp, Royal Troon, during the 1950 British Open?
35. What does 'knee-knocker' mean in golfing terminology?
36. Who was the first Irishman to win the British Open?
37. In what year did Nick Faldo score a hole in one in the Ryder Cup?
38. At what age did Gary Player become the then oldest winner of the US Masters in 1978?
39. Which golfer in 1986 led all four Majors after 54 holes but won only one of them?

40. What is the diameter of a golf hole?

41. Where did Lee Travino chip in on the 71st hole to help him win his second British Open title?

42. In which year was golf dropped from the Olympic Games?

43. On which course would you find the following: The Coffin, Hell Bunker and Ginger Beer?

44. Name the first trophy Gary Player won on British soil.

45. Name the golfer who became the youngest ever Masters champion in 1980.

46. In what year did Jack Nicklaus first compete professionally in Britain?

47. Who was killed by his own club after it was thrown in anger?

48. Who, between 1963 and 1964, devised and played the longest hole in the world, 1 978 720 yards coast to coast across America?

49. Who was the actress and sportswoman who scored a hole in one with her first ever tee shot in her first ever round of golf?

50. Who famously killed a pike with a hooked tee shot at Barnham Broom golf club?

51. Who devoted his life to playing golf on as many courses as possible – 3 615 in total?

52. Who was the professional player who hit 1 817 shots over 16 hours 25 minutes in an attempt to score a hole in one, and failed?

53. Name the only golfer who hit five consecutive shots in the water at the US Masters?

54. Name the only golfer who shot a 63 during a round of the US Masters?

55. Where did Tiger Woods win his first Major?

56. Where was the longest sudden-death playoff in US tour history? It lasted 11 holes.

57. What does the US Masters champion receive?

58. Who won the South African Open in 1991?

59. Who scored a triple, triple, triple, triple bogey during the US Open in 1938?

60. Who carded an 18 on a Par 5 at the Bay Hill Invitational in 1998?

61. Who has finished runner-up the most times at a Major, having never won?

62. Who has missed the cut twice when playing as the defending champion of the US Masters?

63. Who missed a two-foot putt that would have made him the 1989 US Masters champion?

64. Who has appeared seven times in the Ryder Cup for Great Britain but has never finished on the winning team?

65. Which golfer has the nickname 'Huckleberry Dillinger' and said 'Charisma is winning major championships'?

Answers to GOLF TRIVIA on page 123

More Golf Jokes

Four men go golfing. While one heads for the clubhouse to take care of the bill, the others make for the first tee and fill the time bragging about their sons.

'My son is such a successful builder that he gave a friend a new home for free,' says the first.

'My son is a leading car salesman and he earned so much in commission that he was able to give a friend a brand new Mercedes,' brags the second.

'My son is such a brilliant stockbroker that he gave a friend a portfolio of leading shares,' brags the third, as the man who has been settling the bill arrives on the tee.

'We were just talking about how successful our sons are,' says the second man. 'How is yours doing?'

'As you've probably heard,' replies the man, 'he's a prostitute in a gay bar. Even so he seems to be doing very well because just in the last month his lovers have given him a house, a Mercedes and a stock portfolio.'

'Tell me your sins,' says the priest to the man in the confessional.

'Father,' replies the man, 'I've used foul language over the weekend and I feel absolutely awful.'

'What made you use such foul language?'

'Well, I was out golfing with a few of my close buddies. On the first hole I hit a brilliant drive, and as the ball reached the top of its arch a bird swooped and grabbed it right out of the air.'

'Is that when you swore?'

'No, not yet. You see, as the bird landed on the fairway to try to eat the ball, a dog appeared out of nowhere and stole it from the bird and ran off with it.'

'Is that when you swore?'

'No, not yet. You see, the dog ran onto the green and as it passed the hole the green keeper shooed it away,and it dropped the ball in fright about six inches from the hole.'

'Oh! Now I see,' says the priest. 'You missed the f***ing putt, didn't you?'

Answers to GOLF TRIVIA on page 118

1. Gary Player; **2.** Four (1949, 1950, 1952 and 1957); **3.** Three (1961, 1974 and 1978); **4.** 1962 – Arnold Palmer won the US Masters and British Open, Jack Nicklaus won the US Open and Gary Player won the US PGA; **5.** The Kentucky Derby Open in 1958; **6.** 1989; **7.** Tienie Britz in 1972; **8.** David Frost (1989, 1990 and 1992); **9.** Nine; **10.** Fulton Allem in 1988; **11.** Ernie Els, David Frost and Retief Goosen; **12.** 1984 at age 14; **13.** Harry Vardon – six titles; **14.** Tom Morris Snr; **15.** Charles Ward achieved this at St Andrews in 1946; **16.** A replica of the clubhouse at Augusta; **17.** US Masters; **18.** He won the British Open twice (1986 and 1993); **19.** Gary Player in 1965; **20.** He was trailing Hubert Greene by seven strokes and shot a 64 in the final round to claim the title; **21.** Europe and the United States; **22.** Match Play; **23.** Mark James; **24.** Ben Crenshaw; **25.** Peter Butler at the 16th at Muirfield in 1973; **26.** 1973 at Muirfield; **27.** Sergio Garcia; **28.** 14 golf clubs; **29.** John Reid; **30.** Gary Adams in the late 1970s; **31.** The Augusta Club; **32.** Ben Hogan; **33.** 336; **34.** 15; **35.** A very short putt; **36.** Fred Daly; **37.** 1993; **38.** 42; **39.** Greg Norman; **40.** 41/4 inches; **41.** Muirfield; **42.** 1908; **43.** St Andrews; **44.** The Dunlop in 1956; **45.** Seve Ballesteros; **46.** 1962; **47.** Michael Scaglione; **48.** Floyd Scatterlee Rood; **49.** Gertrude Lawrence; **50.** Les King; **51.** Ralph Kennedy; **52.** Harry Gonder; **53.** Tom Weiskopf; **54.** Nick Price; **55.** Augusta – 1997; **56.** At the Motor City Open in 1949; **57.** The Green Jacket; **58.** Wayne Westner; **59.** Ray Ainsley; **60.** John Daly; **61.** Harry Cooper; **62.** Seve Ballesteros; **63.** Scott Hoch; **64.** Tony Jacklin; **65.** Tom Watson

Justplain Darren & Friends Profile
Phil Liggett

Favourite personal sporting memory?	There are many – but mine was winning my first bike race in Southport, England, in 1961. The field came into the last corner and the leaders all fell. I went over the pavement, put my head down and won by a long way. We all need luck!
What's your idea of a perfect weekend?	It never happens, but I would love to wake up in Gordon's Bay, go for an early ride on the bike, then a hike and finish up in a beach bar. The same again on Sunday
What would be the best way for a fan to approach you in a bar?	Quietly – I hate shocks. And if they're female, a kiss would be nice. The guys can buy the first round
What do you refuse to pay for?	Expensive drinks in rip-off bars. Unless someone else is paying
Tell us a secret of your trade?	My notes and biographies – and you're not seeing them!
Have you ever been arrested? And for what?	No – I'm a good boy. Had a few brushes with officials around the world, but still waiting to see the inside of a cell
What's been the lowest task/job you've ever had to perform?	My attitude to life has always been: I'll do anything. I even pushed trolleys around factories serving tea to fat white-collar workers. That has to be down there somewhere
What will always be in your fridge?	A cold bottle of chardonnay and some cheese ... and an empty bottle of milk for those who take their coffee black!
Favourite 'junk food' meal?	None – I have spent too much time in car parks late at night waiting for tapes to be made of television programmes. So the sight of Coke and fries turns me off!
What's the last drink you have before going to bed at night?	Coffee – I can sleep through anything. That is unless someone's offering!
What's your biggest indulgence?	A good pint of English beer – the only thing other countries cannot copy!

Best advice given to you by your mother?	You're not like other boys – you'll be famous one day. I guess she was partially right!
What would your profession be if you were not a professional correspondent?	A zoo keeper or an accountant. I did both soon after leaving school and before I started cycling. I still love animals and that's why I like Africa as a continent
There are Seven Wonders of the World, what's your eighth?	My health – it has given me 40 years of pleasure
Your Top 5 list of music?	Whatever five records are playing at the time! I live next door to a pop star and I was the only one who had never heard of him when he arrived! In fact, I've forgotten his name again. I was brought up in Liverpool near the Cavern, home of the Beatles, Searchers, Hollies, Gerry and the Pacemakers, etc. That was the great period when I would know my music
Best 'chirp' you have heard during a sports event?	'I haven't won the Tour today, but I haven't lost it either.' Stephen Roche in 1987 on Mont Ventoux, who went on to win and become Ireland's only winner of the Tour de France
Who is your mentor/hero?	I don't look up to anyone, but I admire Eddy Merckx, the Belgian legend. I am also never afraid to learn from my peers in the business, as working on TV can be daunting at times
If you could swap places with anyone for a day who would it be, and why?	Myself. I would like to be 20 again with all the bikes I now have and the money, so that I could knock all shades of shit out of those who did it to me then!
A quote or phrase that has had an impact on your life or best describes you?	'The Voice of Cycling'. It was given to me by an Australian commentator at the Commonwealth Games in Auckland, New Zealand, in 1990, and is now used by all the networks around the world
A one-liner that best describes your radio show?	He's a cool guy who knows what his audience wants – more!

Tour de France Trivia

1. What's the highest number of stages won in a single Tour?
2. Which cyclist has won the highest number of stages in their Tour de France career?
3. Who has won the most podium places in their career?
4. What's the highest number of yellow jersey wearers in one Tour?
5. Who has worn the yellow jersey for the most days in their career?
6. What's the biggest winning margin (since 1947)?
7. What's the smallest winning margin?
8. What's the longest sole escape?
9. What's the fastest-ever prologue?
10. What's the fastest time trial?
11. What's the fastest average speed over one stage?
12. What's the fastest average speed over a whole Tour?
13. Who is the oldest-ever winner of the Tour de France?
14. Who is the youngest winner?
15. Who participated in the most Tours (without retiring from a race)?

Answers to TOUR DE FRANCE TRIVIA on page 128

Funny Signs

Sign over a gynaecologist's office: 'Dr Jones, at your cervix.'

On a plumber's truck: 'We repair what your husband fixed.'

At a towing company: 'We don't charge an arm and a leg. We want tows.'

On an electrician's truck: 'Let us remove your shorts.'

On a maternity room door: 'Push. Push. Push.'

In a podiatrist's office: 'Time wounds every heel.'

In a veterinarian's waiting-room: 'Be back in 5 minutes. Sit! Stay!'

At the electric company: 'We would be de-lighted if you send in your bill. However, if you don't, you will be.'

At a radiator shop: 'Best place in town to take a leak.'

The 12 Biggest Lies

12. The cheque is in the mail.

11. You get this one, I'll pay next time.

10. You look great.

9. Of course I love you.

8. It's not the money, it's the principle of the thing.

7. … but we can still be good friends.

6. She means nothing to me.

5. Don't worry, I can go another 20 miles when the gauge is on 'empty'.

4. Don't worry, he's never bitten anyone.

3. I'll call you later.

2. I've never done anything like this before.

1. I DO.

Answers to TOUR DE FRANCE TRIVIA on page 126

1. Eight – by Charles Pelisser (1930), Eddy Merckx (1970, 1974) and Freddy Maertens (1976); **2.** Eddy Merckx – 34 stages; **3.** Raymond Poulidor – eight podium places (three times second, five times third) in 14 Tours, from 1962 to 1976; **4.** Eight, in 1987; **5.** Eddy Merckx – 96 days (in seven Tours); **6.** 28 minutes 27 seconds (Fausto Coppi, Stan Ockers, in 1952); **7.** 8 seconds (Greg LeMond, Laurent Fignon, in 1989); **8.** 253 km by Albert Bourlon in 1947; **9.** 55,152 kph over 7,2 km by Chris Boardman in 1994; **10.** 54.545 kph over 24,5 km by Greg LeMond in 1989; **11.** 50,355 kph over 194,5 km (Laval-Blois) by Mario Cipollini in 1999; **12.** 40,276 kph by Lance Armstrong in 1999; **13.** Firmin Lambot (36) in 1922; **14.** Henri Cornet (20) in 1904; **15.** 16 by Joop Zoetemelk, from 1970 to 1986

Justplain Cocktails

Here are the winners of the Justplain cocktail competition

Shona and Jack

2 shots of Jack
2 shots of vodka
1 tot grenadine
garnish with 2 cherries in a short glass

~

Michael and Jack

1 tot vodka
1 tot Malibu
1 tot banana liqueur
1 tot Jack
1 tot grenadine

~

Johan and Jack

1–2 tots Jack
half shot of Southern Comfort
half shot amaretto/orange juice and grenadine

Justplain Darren & Friends Profile
Aldo Zilli

Favourite personal sporting memory?	Italy winning the World Cup when I was working in a hotel full of Germans … what a scream
What's your idea of a perfect weekend?	Taking my partner on a city break to do some shopping
What would be the best way for a fan to approach you in a bar?	Female – no problem. Male – only if I've had a few drinks and I am watching the football
What do you refuse to pay for?	Parking tickets
Tell us a secret of your trade?	Hard work
Have you ever been arrested? And for what?	Yes, for escaping national service
What's been the lowest task/job you've ever had to perform?	Putting my hand down the toilet
What will always be in your fridge?	Parmesan and tomatoes
Favourite 'junk food' meal?	Chicken burger from Burger King
What's the last drink you have before going to bed at night?	Camomile tea
What's your biggest indulgence?	Pasta and breads

Best advice given to you by your mother?	Do good and forget it, do bad and always worry
What would your profession be if you were not a professional correspondent?	Actor
There are Seven Wonders of the World, what's your eighth?	Sopranos
Your Top 5 list of music?	Rock Pop Classical Opera Jazz
Best 'chirp' you have heard during a sports event?	In 1966 when England won the World Cup, just before final whistle everyone rushed on to the pitch and the commentator went 'They think it is all over' and just then England scored and he said 'It is now'
Who is your mentor/hero?	Frank Sinatra
If you could swap places with anyone for a day who would it be, and why?	Darren Scott because I love working on radio and TV
A quote or phrase that has had an impact on your life or best describes you?	Flamboyant and extrovert
A one-liner that best describes Darren and his radio show?	Witty

Olympic Games Trivia

1. When were the ancient Olympics held?
2. Who won the first ancient Olympic race?
3. Where and when were the first modern Olympic Games held?
4. How many women participated in the first modern Olympics?
5. Who is credited with founding the modern Olympic Games?
6. Which nation won the most medals at the first Modern Olympic Games?
7. What year did the Olympic flag first fly?
8. What year was the Olympic flame introduced?
9. What do the five rings on the Olympic flag represent?
10. In which year were the Olympics first televised?
11. What does the Olympic motto 'Citius, altius, fortius' mean?
12. Where does the Olympic torch-lighting relay begin?
13. Who was the oldest Olympic athlete ever and in what sport did he participate?
14. Who was the youngest Olympic athlete ever?
15. The first ever perfect score 10 in Olympic gymnastics was achieved by Nadia Comaneci in which Olympic Games?
16. Who holds the record for the most individual medals won at the Olympics?
17. In what years have the modern Olympics not been held due to war?
18. In what years did Paris host the Olympic Games?
19. When and where were the first Winter Olympics held?
20. How many gold medals has South Africa won in swimming at the Olympics?

Answers to OLYMPIC GAMES TRIVIA on page 133

A man is out shopping and discovers a new brand of Olympic condoms.

Clearly impressed, he buys a pack. When he gets home he announces to his wife the purchase he just made.

'Olympic condoms?' she blurts.

'Yes,' he says. 'Gold, silver and bronze.'

'What colour are you going to wear tonight?' she asks cheekily.

'Gold, of course,' says the man proudly.

The wife responds, 'Really, why don't you wear silver? It would be nice if you came second for a change!'

Answers to OLYMPIC GAMES TRIVIA on page 132

1. 776 BC and then every 4 years until 339 BC; **2.** Corubus, a chef. He won the sprint of 192 metres (210 yards), which was the length of the stadium; **3.** Athens, Greece, in 1896; **4.** None. (There were 311 male competitors); **5.** Baron Pierre de Coubertin; **6.** Greece; **7.** 1920; **8.** 1932; **9.** The five continents; **10.** 1936 Berlin Games; **11.** 'Swifter, higher, stronger'; **12.** Olympia, Greece; **13.** Oscar Swahn represented Sweden in the shooting category and won his sixth Olympic medal at the 1920 Antwerp Games at the age of 71 years 280 days old; **14.** The youngest ever Olympian is Greek gymnast Dimitrios Loundras, who competed in the 1896 Athens Olympics. He was 10 years old; **15.** The Montreal Olympics in 1976; **16.** Soviet gymnast Larissa Latynina. She competed in three Olympics between 1956 and 1964. She won a total of 18 medals: 9 gold, 5 silver and 4 bronze; **17.** 1916, 1940 and 1944; **18.** 1900 and 1924; **19.** 1924, Chamonix, France; **20.** Three – Joan Harrisson (1952) and Penny Heyns (two in 1996)

Justplain Darren & Friends Profile

John Walland *(seriously, this time)*

Favourite personal sporting memory?	1995 Rugby World Cup final at Ellis Park
What's your idea of a perfect weekend?	A braai with your mates, a few beers, then watch a rugby match on TV at home
What would be the best way for a fan to approach you in a bar?	Introduce yourself and move on
What do you refuse to pay for?	Water
Tell us a secret of your trade?	Perseverance and dedication
Have you ever been arrested? And for what?	No
What's been the lowest task/job you've ever had to perform?	Stapling tyre labels every night for a month, for a bicycle
What will always be in your fridge?	Milk
Favourite 'junk food' meal?	Kentucky Fried Chicken
What's the last drink you have before going to bed at night?	Water
What's your biggest indulgence?	Food and exercise

Best advice given to you by your mother?	
What would your profession be if you were not a professional radio presenter?	TV presenter
There are Seven Wonders of the World, what's your eighth?	Life
Your Top 5 list of music?	1 U2 2 Fleetwood Mac 3 Ronan Keating 4 Creed 5 Kylie Minogue
Best 'chirp' you have heard during a sports event?	The batsman's Holding, the bowler's Willey.
Who is your mentor/hero?	Nelson Mandela
If you could swap places with anyone for a day who would it be, and why?	Justplain – give him some of his own medicine, for a laugh
A quote or phrase that has had an impact on your life or best describes you?	Live well for today, for yesterday is but a dream and tomorrow just a vision. Success is not defined by obtaining everything you want, but by appreciating everything you have.
A one-liner that best describes Darren and his radio show?	Brilliant, polished and professional